THE GAME CHANGER

VOL. 2

Inspirational Stories That Changed Lives

BY
IMAN AGAY • ARROW GONSALVES • BEN PRITCHETT
BRADY PATTERSON • CHUCK SUTHERLAND
JAMIE SULLIVAN • JANAK MEHTA • KRYS PAPPIUS
LINDA A. OLSON • LISE LAVIGNE • MARILYN SUTHERLAND
PAT IYER • QUYNH VO • SUSAN BINNIE

The Game Changer (Volume 2): Inspiring Stories That Changed Lives
© 2018 by Success Road Enterprises. All rights reserved.

No part of this publication may be reproduced, distributed, or transmitted in any form or by any means, including photocopying, recording, or other electronic or mechanical methods, without the prior written permission of the publisher, except in the case of brief quotations embodied in critical reviews and certain other non-commercial uses permitted by copyright law.

Ordering Information:
Copies of this book may be ordered directly from:
www.mylifechangingmoment.com

Website: **www.mychangingmoment.com**
Cover Illustration Copyright © 2018 by George Ramsis
Cover Design by George Ramsis
Published by Success Road Enterprises
eBook ISBN 978-0-9948108-7-8

This book is intended to provide information only. The information contained in this book is not meant for professional purposes. This book is sold with the understanding that neither the author nor the publisher is responsible for providing any legal or other professional services published in this book. Personal circumstances are different with everyone; because of this, individuals need to seek professional advice for their own personal health. The authors specifically disclaim any liability, loss or risk that is incurred as a consequence directly or indirectly, of the use or application of any of the contents of this work. The opinions in this book are of the authors' and do not reflect the opinions of any outside group.

Although every precaution has been taken to verify the accuracy of the information contained herein, the author and the publisher assume no responsibility for any errors or omissions. No liability is assumed for damages that may result from the use of the information contained within.

Table of Contents

Introduction by Iman Aghay..1

Arrow Gonsalves: Into the Mystic......................................3

Ben Pritchett: Never Give Up...17

Brady Patterson: Phoenix Rising.....................................33

Chuck Sutherland: The Secret That Changed My Life Forever.......41

Jamie Sullivan: A Gentle Way: Intuition and Business Unite........51

Janak Mehta: An Immigrant's Journey to Feedom and Fortune....59

Krys Pappius: Surviving the Perfect Storm......................67

Linda A. Olson: An Entrepreneurial Dream......................79

Lise Lavigne: 50 Shades of Wrong....................................89

Marilyn Sutherland: My Journey to Lasting Love.......................101

Pat Iyer: From Near Bankruptcy to Millions...................113

Quynh Vo: Never Good Enough................................127

Susan Binnie: You Say You Can't?...Think Again!........................143

Quotes from "The Game Changer," vol. 2
Inspirational Stories that Changed Lives

"Suddenly a portal into my deeper reality opened. The stark truth of my situation coursed through my entire system and engulfed me in despair. Despite all my ability, talent and potential, I knew in my bones that I was going down and this time I really might not have the strength to get back up. In a state of shock, I became acutely aware of how recklessly I'd squandered my energy."

-Arrow Gonsalves, "Into the Mystic"

Never Give Up!
"If you're going through hell, keep going"
–Winston Churchill
"My wife looked at me with tears in her eyes and said, "Are you thinking of doing something stupid? I'd rather be poor with you, than wealthy without you."

-Ben Pritchett- Never Give Up!

"If it weren't for this night, things would be much different for me. That night was my turning point. That was the catalyst to trigger me to quit smoking, drugs, and alcohol in one day, cold turkey . It wasn't an easy task, but I finally understood what impact my environment had on me."

Brady Patterson – "Phoenix Rising"

"I was sitting in the dark on the floor of my bedroom, suffering, crying, and blaming. I felt totally broken. "Why? Why? Why is this happening to me?" I asked that question over and over again!

Suddenly, sitting there in the dark, I had this massive realization that continues to change my life to this day!"
Chuck Sutherland – I Discovered a Huge Secret that Changed My Life Forever

"Even though I'd had my confidence pummeled about what was possible for me as an entrepreneur, I knew if I was yearning to express myself in business "that" way, it's because it was possible. In the centre of my dream board was/is a picture of a big beautiful tree sprinkled with twinkle lights against the backdrop of night, and a white snowy ground."

    Jamie Sullivan – A Gentle Way: Intuition & Business Unite

"Looking back, it was a crash course in growing up in the entrepreneurial world. I t was not easy, and I do not recommend this roller-coaster ride for the faint-hearted. I am glad that I have a wonderfully supportive wife who has stood by my side through the thick and thin!

I want to end this chapter with my gratitude towards my family, friend, and this country. I believe that you get second chances in very few places in this world and this is one of those places. So, if an immigrant with a dream and determination can make it in this country; you can too! Never Give up and Make it Happen!!!"

    Janak Mehta – An Immigrants Journey to Freedom and Fortune

"As this collision was unfolding, my life literally flashed before my eyes, and at that moment, I felt a great deal of sadness, sadness because I knew that if I did not survive this event, my life would have meant very little. I was not leaving any legacy of value. I had not made a difference."

    Krys Pappius – Surviving the Perfect Storm

"Two months later, I faced one of the most difficult days of my life as she walked me through in slow motion the worst day of my life – the day we lost little Billy. I sobbed from such depths I didn't know if I would ever recover. My therapist didn't want me to drive home in this emotional state so had me wait in another room."

    Linda A. Olson – An Entrepreneurial Dream

The Game Changer

"My actions were out of love and a need to please the man I loved and desired. I was successful at making that happen. I didn't care about my own feelings in doing it. I overstepped on my values to please another and disregarded my intuition and ignored my inner guidance to accomplish this. I pleased another by having no respect for myself."

Lise Lavigne – 50 Shades of Wrong

"My big insight? I was actively rejecting love that didn't match my expectations. I said I wanted a life filled with love yet, when love showed up; I had pushed it away. Where else had I pushed love away because it didn't match my expectations?"

Marilyn Sutherland – My Journey to Lasting Love

"I felt my body tremble as I was ushered into the office of the Dean of the School of Nursing of the University of Pennsylvania I attended. It seemed like the office was the size of a football field. I eased into the chair opposite the dean's desk and took a deep breath."

Pat Iyer – From Near Bankruptcy to Millions

"I was kicked out of Pharmacy school because my mark was too low. It was a sentence that was more mortifying to me than death. At least, if I had died, I'd only have to suffer that one moment in time, and then that's it. But now, I have to live with this consequence, and I have to tell my mom."

Quynh Vo – Never Good Enough

"None of this was planned, life was not supposed to be this way. I had no time to think, sleep or breathe. I was upset every moment and just wanted to curl up into a ball and cry. Finally, after five very long and emotional weeks, she was strong enough to come home, strong enough to be the nor¬mal little girl that would have a perfect life, the life I had planned for her."

Susan Binnie – You Say You Can't? …Thing Again! can too! Repeat after me…YES, I CAN!

Iman Aghay

INTRODUCTION

I've been working with entrepreneurs and other successful professionals for the past 16 years. Working as a business mentor, I often get to see the complex interworking of an entrepreneur's life. I get the privilege of hearing about what goes on behind the scenes. I can't tell you how humbling it is to know what it takes for entrepreneurs to realize their achievements.

The Game Changer Book Series is a collection of these behind the scene stories. Stories that most people never consider behind a business or successful company. These stories are personal, connected to the authors' hearts, and many of them are being shared for the first time with you, our reader. While I was reading this collection, I could not stop thinking about this old adage: "Everyone you meet is fighting a battle you know nothing about! Be kind, always…"

This book reveals some of the hardest times and the darkest moments that entrepreneurs live through. These are real and deeply personal experiences. Many of the chapters are about making bad choices and overcoming mistakes. But all of them share something in common: a turning point. The turning point that changed the author's life forever. These stories are very dear to each author, and I am honoured to be able to share their experiences with you. I hope that each of these stories touches you the way that they have touched me.

– ImanAghay

The Game Changer

ARROW GONSALVES
Into The Mystic

I returned to the "Way" in Boston, Massachusetts. I can pinpoint the moment I began my desperate search for reconnection. It was September 2000, three o'clock on a weekday afternoon, and I was sitting alone in an expensive suit staring down the scene of a long, dimly lit bar.

Suddenly a portal into my deeper reality opened. The stark truth of my situation coursed through my entire system and engulfed me in despair. Despite all my ability, talent and potential, I knew in my bones that I was going down and this time I really might not have the strength to get back up. In a state of shock, I became acutely aware of how recklessly I'd squandered my energy.

I'd been living and working in the US for 12 years, along with my son and husband. I had a successful wholesale business and a wonderful lifestyle travelling the Eastern seaboard. Under the surface though, everything was in turmoil. My once charming and charismatic husband was 16 months into a two-year jail sentence. My will had completely dissolved. I was drinking daily to numb the pain and could not stop. With horror, I realized I was in worse condition than my husband, whom I'd fought so hard to save. I felt I had no one to turn to for help, despite a lifetime of proving I could overcome any obstacle. Now my daily life felt like an endurance test that would never end. My power depleted, I was staring into a dark future. My business that I loved and had built up from nothing was also slipping away. At this rate, I would soon be impoverished and alone in a foreign country.

How that one deeply despairing moment transformed me into one of the most blessed and fortunate women in the world, living in paradise with a vibrant community of students and vision partners, amazes me to this day. It was a humbling time. I held the raw desperation of that moment as one would grip a clifftop overhanging a precipice and sought help with all my might, albeit with the strength of a confused, drowning mouse. I went daily to AA and started to feel some optimism in taking small progressive actions. Within weeks, though still befuddled, I felt stronger and desired a deeper engagement with myself.

I was intrigued by yoga because I'd heard it could restore balance. Yoga appealed to me because I had spent my life continuously driving myself to do everything well: eating well, daily exercise, striving for business success. This desire to learn meditation and restore balance soon led me to my beloved teacher Master Chun Shim, where my path of returning to empowerment with the Tao began.

I remember walking into Chun Shim's healing studio in Boston for our initial consultation, unsure what to expect. There was a clear, tranquil quality in the ambiance, a twinkle in Chun Shim's eyes and great warmth in her manner, which revealed a depth of wisdom I'd never encountered before.

During that session, Chun Shim so adeptly re-sparked my hope and sense of adventure I signed up for her entire package of workshops and classes. I recognized that this was the moment to seize my healing chance with all my being. I started surrendering all that was not true to uncover my true self and began living my life with increased meaning. As I restored balance physically, I strengthened my drive and observed my attachments to unhealthy behaviours dissolve. Within months I felt joyful, regained a level of confidence and was no longer controlled by pain. Little did I know the phenomenal adventure that beckoned from igniting that little spark.

I felt an instant resonance between my personality and interests and the methodology of the Tao Healing Arts. It is in its essence a nature-based philosophy and physical process of steadily cultivating and managing one's energy to create harmony in body, mind, and spirit. The techniques restore core strength and self-connection and gradually awaken greater awareness, so that leadership emerges along with one's charisma and the confidence to activate a greater life purpose. During my process of awakening, the method underlying these ancient practises systematically revealed how to revitalize myself from within, while questioning the reasons and meaning of life and my existence.

This paradigm was an ideal fit for me because I had always been physically active and fascinated with the brain, universal law and the ways of nature. My father was a Brain Specialist and the first operator of the CTVS (CAT scan). He ran several Canadian university and hospital neurology departments. My mother was a social worker and horticulturist whose father was a pharmacist in London during the days of traditional compounding. On a spiritual level, I've always felt most connected to the higher power inherent in nature.

About five months after beginning my practise, when I awakened my soul, I realized that I am love. I saw the root of my dysfunction: my past idea of love came from neediness based on yearning, endurance and proving my worth with perfectionism. Through new insights, I determined to keep on this path to empowerment by sincere daily training, prayer, and meditation.

Through my journeys in sacred landscapes of North America, I discovered my soul's purpose that guides me to this day. I'm driven to share the story of this awakening and how I began to unfold my most creative, meaningful life. I offer forward what I've learned as another way of fostering the health of society by helping people awaken their consciousness as they restore health.

During this period, I trained my brain and body daily, seeking truth and clarity. I felt strong and centered. People commented that I looked years younger. As I learned the nature of attachments, my desire to become an instrument channeling love and light deepened. I began wondering what this might actually entail and whether I had the gumption to surrender so deeply. But once I uncovered my vision, I challenged myself to give everything I had. I determined to put both my faith and the methodology to the test.

One day several years into my practice, I was holding a training posture that induces deep meditation, and finally started unfolding my long sought for vision. At first, I envisioned a property outside Vanderhoof in Northern British Columbia. I knew it was a healing center and understood I was to work with First Nations communities there.

Over the next year I fleshed out my plans, finally left my husband and steadily continued to intensify my training program. I started planning my return to Canada to put my vision into action. After 15 long years in Boston, I left on the labour-day weekend of 2005, ready to leave the nest and fly.

I made a final visit to the studio to share a fond farewell with my Healer Trainer, Master Hong. While outlining my plans, a voice surfaced from deep inside and resounded through me, saying, "When the First Nations heal, their vibration will heal North America." My eyes opened wide in surprise. Master Hong cried, and we hugged. I realized I wasn't picturing the Canadian region of Vanderhoof but Hazelton, another village in Northern BC that I knew from earlier days. Hazelton is a Gitxsan village set deep in a natural bowl surrounded by towering mountains. Among First Nations, its inhabitants are known as "the people of the Mist."

Arrow Gonsalves: Into the Mystic

I aimed my big U-Haul truck westbound on route 90 and set off. I felt excited and a bit melancholy, aware that I wouldn't see many people I loved again, including my husband, friends, and clients I'd collected over the past 15 years.

Midway on my journey, as I entered South Dakota, I felt irresistibly pulled to find a spot to stop and meditate. This halfway point seemed like a fitting place to say goodbye to the past and turn fully to the future. I pulled into a Tourist Center to inquire about nearby highlights.

A Native American woman greeted me and mentioned that the next day (Labor Day) there would be a big celebration to commemorate the 75th anniversary of the Crazy Horse Monument. The date also marked the anniversaries of the death of Crazy Horse and birth of Korczak Ziolkowski, the Polish carver who took on the ambitious task of carving the famous war hero's image into one of the Black Hills.

I voiced uncertainty since I was just looking for a quick diversion and not intending to stay overnight. But the woman insisted this was a must-see event. She told me plainly, "The Crazy Horse Monument makes Mount Rushmore look like a postage stamp." It just wasn't as well known because the carver wouldn't let it become a national monument. He felt it should remain private to honour the Sioux Nation that asked him to do the project.

I took a brochure and left, determined to follow a quick loop off the main highway through the Badlands and then continue my way to Canada. This is not how the journey unfolded.

I can only describe the next three days as surreal. I felt I'd entered a mystic portal. Time slowed, and a yearning ache from deep within guided me. I felt driven to seek spots to meditate, as I needed to extract some elusive essence from the center of my meditations in this powerful location.

Softly and seductively, the tall grasses lining the tops of the Badlands gently

The Game Changer

whispered the language of the ancestors as I followed a nearly magnetic pull of energy. I zigzagged across the region from the Crazy Horse Museum and Monument to Bear Butte (a sacred place known as the heart of North America where great leaders such as Black Elk, Sitting Bull and many others did their vision quests), to the Memorial of the Battle of Little Big Horn. In the process, I gained great insights. I connected to the spirits of the ancients, the little spark that I felt remaining deep within the Tree of Life, and the need for Native Women to heal and have their voices once again heard in Council.

The moment after receiving one last message at the memorial, the portal closed. I was instantly back in my usual state and ready to continue my way west. But my new understandings carried me on, serving to fire my inspiration.

I understood now in energetic terms that there were three key geographic areas in North America, one already activated in Sedona, Arizona. I realized that by sharing the energy practices I'd learned in Boston farther north, I would help light a spark of enlightenment with the Gitxsan people. When this spark took, the heartland would open through the Dakota Sioux, and the resulting vibration would radiate outward through the continent. As wild as this seems, it makes sense on several dimensions. It is analogous to the physical process of enlightenment, which involves activating and harmonizing the three primary internal energy centers, known as the 2nd, 4th, and 6th chakras.

After arriving in the southern interior of BC, I took a little cabin by a mountaintop lake and went into a two-year isolation, focused on building intellectual capital and personal preparation. I'd take to the road for several weeks, travelling through BC and Alberta to build my wholesale business. I kept to myself, walking forest paths, working and training every day for hours. I'd then return to my homestead for weeks of solitude.

One year while researching a trip to Sedona, where I intended to return to complete my Master-Level Healer training, I made a surprising discovery.

Arrow Gonsalves: Into the Mystic

The group I'd trained with, in Boston, had purchased a 4000-acre ranch as an international training and meditation retreat center, south of Vanderhoof in Northern BC, in the exact place I'd seen during my vision in Boston years before.

The coincidences didn't end there. As I located the property on a map, I realized the Nechako River ran through the property. This is the river where I had directed my son to scatter my ashes some 15 years earlier, as we prepared to move to Boston. I later learned that the group had purchased the property during Labour Day weekend 2005 - the same weekend I was engulfed in my adventure in South Dakota. So, in the spring of 2007, I traveled to the retreat centre. I quickly decided to close my business and move in.

This represented another challenging and highly mystical time for me. As a Canadian living in a Korean community in a traditional hermitage, I had an ideal opportunity to step back and observe my mind and ego. I was able to maintain my purpose and retreated within the language barrier, although as my senses sharpened, I could understand much of what was said, and vice versa. I loved exploring new dimensions of the practices, including experimenting with fasting and silent training that lasted months.

This was a time for me to slip into a stage of invisibility that ultimately lasted another seven years. Although I looked bland on the surface, I enjoyed an amazingly vibrant inner world of prayer and wild manifestation that seemed to synchronize with the moon, sun, and clouds and drew unusual activity from birds and wildlife. Layer by layer, the sharp edges of my character rose to the surface to be worn smooth and swept away. I followed the uncharted landscape of my mind with only the principles, method and my faith to guide me.

Several years later, I left the hermitage and traveled west to Hazelton to activate my mission. I was broke, aside from a generous $1,000 loan from another practitioner at the retreat centre.

The Game Changer

I found a decent rate in a decrepit motel before spending most of my remaining funds on a small furnished room. I lived on a tiny bit of rice and vegetables while finding my way around the surrounding villages, creating all the alliances and opportunities I could to begin teaching Tao Yoga.

My communication skills were rusty after spending so much time at the retreat centre with few opportunities to communicate in English. Nevertheless, key matriarchs drew in as they recognized the practises were helping awaken something deep within. Before long I had a loyal crew. Their friends and families witnessed and wanted to share in the ripple effects of positive changes.

Within two months I converted a large space that was once the local drugstore on the main street and opened my first studio, the Sun Tao Center in Hazelton. My bed consisted of a sleeping bag and yoga mat in the studio's back room. I had cold running water and showered at the laundromat.

I visited Health Centers, First Nations' band offices and nursing stations, raising funds and creating offers for open memberships for all band members at a very low rate. I was far more interested in finding people to train to accomplish my mission than charging fair value at the time.

I led classes from my studio and travelled twice weekly to nearby Moricetown to teach in gymnasiums and classrooms. The Gitxsan and Wet'suwet'en people were some of the most sensitive, tender-hearted people I'd ever had the grace to meet. I loved and treasured my students and was delighted as a core group of determined change-makers formed and grew.

I felt honoured that my work was important and much needed, as the flip side of the people's amazingly soft nature seems to show up in a pain body which is so large and raw that it's overwhelming for many. The community feels as one heart and one mind, and when one suffers, gets sick or dies the broader community grieves, feeling it deeply.

Arrow Gonsalves: Into the Mystic

It was beautiful to glimpse the depth and intertwining nature of the community's roots in their ancestors and their land. The same families have been living, working and sharing good and bad times throughout their region for over a thousand years.

Living there, I was in a deep state of mysticism, which kept me on track and guided the steps of my strategy. Initially, there was a period of challenge and testing from what seemed to be all angles. Some of my First Nations friends offered to perform a cleansing ceremony, solemnly clearing the unwelcome energies to brighter and higher levels. The more I honoured and deeply engaged with the region, the more I felt the ancestors' presence assuring me.

I recall sitting by a gorge in meditation when suddenly I was struck by the region's abundance. Cradled within tall and rugged mountains, the fertile valleys contain fish, and forests are brimming with rich soil, wildlife, edible plants, and medicines. From this perspective of this natural richness, it saddened me that there, like everywhere, people were as chained as they were bedazzled by the promise of modernity's so-called creature comforts. It's even more painfully striking when seen from a place of injustice and lack.

I decided that one avenue of my healing work would come through a children's program based on the same methodology I use, the Tao Healing Arts. Recognizing the critical role it could play in the long term, I invited collaboration from the International Brain Education Association (IBREA).

Together we trained 42 school teachers, mental health personnel and band youth workers from the surrounding region in a 12-lesson program delivered as a school curriculum. I then offered the program through my studio as an opportunity for the instructors to teach it collectively. It was a wonderful success. Parents shared how their children brought home the practices. They saw results not only in the child but in the whole family.

The Game Changer

A mother contacted me to express appreciation and told the story of her brother dying the previous weekend. Finding her sobbing, the woman's seven-year-old son gently shared a technique that calmed her and helped her process the waves of emotion. She was amazed how that one beautiful act bonded the family and changed the energy of the home.

As the energy of the studio grew, people commented that the town center felt brighter. Little reassurances started surfacing that the environment was changing, especially within the lives of my students and their families. As is the way with the Tao, there was energy at work on the subtle realms that co-existed alongside my physical efforts. Over time I was invited to participate in various sweat lodges presided over by the region's small handful of pipe carriers traditionally trained in that plain's style of ceremony.

One held particularly special significance. Pipe Carrier Shari Martin invited four others and me to honour life and offer prayers for light and healing. We came together in the woods on a fresh autumn morning, and each took our turn in song and heartfelt expression. I prayed silently for Creator to awaken the light of the people and activate the healing energy of my vision. I shared in coarser terms than my more eloquent companions, but as I completed my expression, I felt a white light in the shape of a soft cloud, like stardust, swirl outward, around and up through the sweat lodge. I knew my prayer was heard and something had taken hold.

As word of the Sun Tao Center spread, a small group of Healing Touch practitioners from Prince Rupert started to cross the 200-mile distance for workshops. Their central figure was an influential woman who assured me of my welcome in Prince Rupert once my time in Hazelton was complete. Other than instruction, I continued to spend my time in self-imposed isolation. Through that winter I started to feel I'd spiraled to the bottom of a bowl, which in essence I literally had. My studio was located in the lowest part of the valley formed by the rivers and high mountains. My mind had also spiralled inward for seven years, and I started to feel quagmired.

Events triggered a period of deep grieving. One day while walking my dog by the river I sat inside a hollowed-out totem pole that formed the doorway to the village feast-house, and up surfaced a chant of mourning. I chanted it seven times, as done formally when releasing the spirit from grief. Midway through the 4th rendition, I witnessed the sacred ancestors of nearby Mount Sdikyoodenax and the ancestral energy of my practice, Dangun, surface in the sky (really my 6th chakra). The energies nodded to each other and merged. When completed I opened my eyes and saw the energy of the two rivers that joined beyond the treeline in front of me, merging and flowing steadily to the ocean, as do we all when we are ready.

Within months I had trained three instructors to continue classes. I bid farewell to my beloved students and the ancestors and followed the road alongside the river, gratefully accepting the invitation to Prince Rupert. I arrived exhausted and spent.

By then I knew I ultimately wanted to move to Vancouver Island to build a lasting base and business foundation. I also knew I needed a period of gentle immersion into society before I could handle such intensity.

Prince Rupert was ideal for this purpose. A small group of enthusiastic people welcomed me and joined classes. I put together a beautiful studio space in the museum, a traditional Yellow Cedar Longhouse with massive columns, overlooking the ocean. I turned my mind to fleshing out my programs and curriculum.

One young student, a local web designer, offered to tutor me to build a website in exchange for training. He was keen and had a challenging time managing his considerable energy. Through the exercises and meditations, he was able to harness his mind and develop the ability for focused concentration. He walked through his fears and realized how deeply he wanted to make a difference in his town and the world. He started a local Transition Town initiative and within three years had become Prince Rupert's mayor, drawing the highest municipal voter turnout in local history and receiving just over 50% of the vote.

The Game Changer

After taking office, Lee wrote to me: "Thank you Arrow, – if it wasn't for your guidance that put me on the path within and helped me develop my daily practice – I would never have reached the truth inside. I wish you well on your new journey and trust that I will see you again when the time is right. Thank you for being an amazing teacher." This always inspires me. The ripple effect of Lee's work is making important inroads toward a more enlightened and healthy society on the Canadian Northwest Coast.

I remained in Prince Rupert for two years before I felt ready to journey south to Vancouver Island. Again, I trained a few instructors to carry on with classes and take over the studio.

I chose Courtenay in the Comox Valley because it has all the ingredients to be a role model of a resilient and sustainable society. We have a vibrant agricultural community with some of the best soils in the region and a long growing season. From the iconic glacier that straddles the mountain range, to the coastal estuaries and rivers that support salmon, forests and local economies, this area has been known by the K'omoks First Nation as a land of plenty for countless generations. My task is to help spark the creative fire of self-connection that facilitates more wisdom, adaptability, harmony, and collaboration. I knew this was the place I could hone my vision of awakening change-makers for the greater whole.

I gutted a large space in Downtown Courtenay and opened what is now a flourishing wellness center called, "The House of Now." I sublet the training room to other instructors and have five treatment rooms in the clinic side which are fully booked with a skilled group of professionals.

I offer adventurous self-development retreats in beautiful locations and have a solid client base both regionally and online. Currently, I'm writing a book titled: "The Way of the Tao - A Mystic's Adventure Serving the Divine." I do regular public speaking engagements and recently participated in one of the largest TED Talks conferences in the world to engage the audience with a customized "Audience Energizer."

Arrow Gonsalves: Into the Mystic

Looking back on that terrifying moment of awakening in Boston and the struggle and confusion of that time in my life, I see it as a great blessing. While your story and personal goals may differ in intensity, we all grow our souls and characters in this way, by turning the mind within and walking forward with faith, courage, and determination. The greater and more mindful your goal, and the more limitations you overcome to develop your character, the more you will grow in wisdom and compassion and benefit the whole.

I view life as a grand adventure fed by my sense of purpose and work that nourishes my soul. I live in paradise, inspiring people to step forward with confidence and purpose, among a community of amazingly creative, caring and resilient people who are making real change in the world. It really is a dream coming true.

As you live your life, I hope you create meaningful purpose that fuels your passion. I wish with all my heart that you're inspired to turn your mind within and dare to dream the dream that will awaken your full potential. You can hone your brain and body to give life everything you've got and create a legacy that benefits you, your community and the entire planet.

If there's one thing I know - it's that **YOU CAN DO IT!**

ABOUT THE AUTHOR

ARROW GONSALVES is the Founder of Human Energetics and Owner of Heart Drum Beat - Brain & Body Training Academy and The House of Now Wellness Center.

She is a Master Trainer | Master Healer in the Tao Healing Arts, a public speaker, audience energizer and internationally published author.

Since 2003 Arrow has trained individuals who want to be more healthy, focused and productive, guiding students to strengthen their character by connecting to their core and challenging them to heal and reach for their fullest potential in life.

Her live in-studio and online classes, retreats and workshops encourage empowerment and mindful living by systematically cultivating the internal Qi Energy system through Meridian Exercise, Chakra Training, Brain Education, and dynamic and static forms of chant and meditation. As students harmonize and cultivate their inner nature, charismatic leadership qualities emerge and the Laws of Attraction align with their deeper goals, helping them achieve their higher purpose.

*2017 TEDX Stanley Park Energizer
Email: arrow@heartdrumbeat.com
www.heartdrumbeat.com
https://www.linkedin.com/in/arrow-gonsalves
https://www.facebook.com/heartdrumbeat
https://twitter.com/ArrowGonsalves

BEN PRITCHETT
Never Give Up!

"If you're going through hell, keep going"
—Winston Churchill

My wife looked at me with tears in her eyes and said, "Are you thinking of doing something stupid? I'd rather be poor with you, than wealthy without you."

I'm not sure how this women's intuition thing works (I am a guy after all), but what I do know is that our businesses had been dealt one blow after another for a couple of years, and I couldn't see a way out. What I did know was that I had a negative (or very low) net worth alive, but I was worth about $3 million dead.

That was enough to cover all our corporate debts with money left over. It would set my family up for life, and I felt that was more important than anything else. I'd done everything else I could do and thought this made the most sense.

To be clear, for me this was a business decision. I wasn't overly happy, but I wasn't depressed either. It wasn't a quick rash decision; it had come together over several weeks because I wanted to fix our problems while inconveniencing the fewest people possible. I had a wife and daughter that I loved more than I loved myself, so their comfort and well-being was the most important thing to me.

I am a planner, always have been. I've written a bestselling book on building systems in businesses. Everything is step-by-step. I think of things like a chess game. I have to make my moves while trying to determine what my opponents' next moves will be. I make no claims of being a grandmaster, but it is said that they can see 10 or 12 moves into a game. I'm not bad, but I'm not that good either.

This was a very complicated game of chess though, there was more than one opponent, more than one board, and I was blindfolded half the time. There was a bad partnership, a couple of failing business, a very duplicitous (or possibly just incompetent at that time) bank, and a slew of other issues swirling around me all at once.

Between 2008 and 2010 it seemed that no matter what I touched, it turned to shit (and that's being generous). This was true for business ventures and some personal issues as well.

Although things certainly hadn't always run silky smooth (we'd weathered more than our share of problems), we'd managed to achieve considerable success between 2003 and 2005, with three successful optometry clinic acquisitions (my wife's profession), and welcomed a beautiful baby girl into our family in 2007.

The problems started the week our daughter was born. The day after we got her home from the hospital, we had a meeting with our banker at our dining room table. After a successful collaboration over four years and three successful practice acquisitions, (Stonewall, Swan River, and Winnipeg – all in Manitoba) he was changing jobs and passing us over to a new account manager. I should have run screaming from the house then.

Ben Pritchett: Never Give Up!

I was assured that the bank was extremely pleased with our progress to date, it had our backs and would continue to support our growth. He went so far as to tell me that we had essentially earned a "blank cheque" from the bank going forward. It was a blank cheque alright; there was nothing on it. Things really started to unravel in 2008.

I decided to start a business brokerage, and we were about to acquire our largest clinic to date (our second location in Winnipeg). Oh yes, we also decided to add to our family (when I met my wife, she wanted six kids – no kidding – and I was shooting for two.) I'd negotiated her down to three and was still working on her for two.

Despite a promise to refinance our practices to help with future acquisitions and a building purchase, they ended up lending us 65% of what they had promised. We could live with it though – it was difficult, but we tightened our belts, and things were going okay until we pursued the new acquisition.

I submitted a business plan and was told that I had the bank's support as presented. Then, after we were past-the point of no return on the deal, the bank gutted us by reducing our loan by 20% and the term of the loan by 30%. We ended up with less money and practically the same payments. The bank specifically cut the loan by our entire marketing budget, and actually told me that a business like ours didn't need marketing.

We battened down the hatches and prepared to weather the storm. Shortly after our deal financed, the capital markets collapsed in the US, and Canadian banks stopped lending too. My business brokerage venture was destroyed (although it took me a couple of years to sign the death warrant). The new optometry practice went from bad to worse.

We had two partners in the new optometry practice, but after barely a year the smaller partner decided to walk away and return his shares, leaving us in a 50-50 scenario. Let me say it now; I don't recommend that anybody reading this ever enter into a 50-50 business arrangement without an ironclad dispute resolution mechanism!

The Game Changer

But, I digress a little. The other partner in the practice began acting erratically. He refused to sign off on financial statements (so we couldn't even file a tax return). He wouldn't sign lease renewal documents that nearly cost the business to lose all its equipment. He refused to lay off staff who were no longer needed and even hired additional staff when the business was hemorrhaging money daily.

While our businesses were suffering, we were also trying to add to our family without success. We'd had our first child quite normally, so there was no expectation of problems the second time around. No such luck, and no medical explanation. We decided to skip the line in Canada and pursue IVF in the US. After two attempts and $40,000, a second child was not to be.

This was very frustrating and emotionally draining. The doctors only managed to harvest three eggs throughout this process in 2009, and only two of those proved viable. Despite being successfully fertilized and implanted, neither egg resulted in pregnancy. My belief is that life begins at fertilization, and I mourn the loss of those two babies to this day.

When it became obvious that a baby of our own was not in the cards we pursued adoption, but this was also a fruitless effort, and we stopped trying to adopt in 2015. We have one great child though and are very blessed to have her.

Back to the business saga though…

We were pouring money into the company from our successful practices to the tune of tens of thousands of dollars. Without formal financial statements, we couldn't even try to refinance. However, I had been careful to structure the corporations so that our successful practices weren't linked to the failing partnership.

By this time, I was very concerned, and the bank was starting to breathe down our necks. I'd begun taking a friend to all bank meetings under the guise of him being an adviser, just so we could pick apart the meeting after, and see if he'd heard what I'd heard because we'd been misled so many times. Without a single exception, the bank representative (we had yet another account manager) said one thing, and the bank did something else.

In December of 2010, we met with the bank once again. Our account manager informed us that the bank was aware of all we had been doing to support our problem practice and that the bank was going to help us fix the problem. He explained that they would be refinancing our successful practices and putting the problem practice into something known as "special loans." That, dear readers, is the banking equivalent of purgatory.

At the end of February in 2011, our account manager called and told me that they were not going to refinance the successful practices and were, in fact, going to put all the companies into special loans. This was even though there was no cross-collateralization in place. Our lines of credit were cut, and other credit was frozen. It seriously looked like the end for us.

It was around this time that I finalized my plan to save our businesses, save our employees their jobs and make sure that my wife and daughter had the resources to enjoy life…even if it had to be without me. It would be business financing via life insurance, and I felt it was worth it with everything else on the line.

My reasoning was that with all the debt gone there would be plenty of cash flow to hire somebody to run the businesses in my place. I'd always sought to give my wife a plan should something happen to me. She knew who to turn to for advice, and she knew the type of person that I would hire to replace me. It was set.

I wish I knew the exact date, but I do not. All I know is that we were talking, and some inner voice must have told her what I was planning to do, and that's when she said, "You aren't thinking about doing something stupid are you? I'd rather be poor with you, than wealthy without you."

I don't mean to make light of this; it was a devastating time. I had plenty to live for, but I felt an overbearing responsibility to provide for my family and the many employees who depended upon us for their livings. When my wife busted me, I promised that I wouldn't carry out my plan and vowed to fight on.

I'd love to tell you that the clouds parted and the sun shone down on us the next day, and everything went swimmingly well from there, but it did not. In most ways, it went from bad to worse.

Three weeks later we found out that the doctor at our most Northern practice in Swan River, Manitoba, was opening accounts and preparing to open a competing practice in a small town and market of only 18,000 people. This woman had been my wife's friend from her optometry school days…in fact, we'd rescued her and her husband from potential bankruptcy and set them up at our practice. What a repayment!

I could write a book just on what happened there alone, but suffice it to say we took massive action to save our best practice. We wrote her termination letter that afternoon and drove the 5 hours to the clinic. We met the doctor there the next morning, terminated her employment with us on the spot, and my wife saw her patients that day and the next.

We were living in Stonewall at the time. Over the next 10 weeks (from March 23rd to June 1st), we sold our house and a piece of land that we had planned to build our dream house on, packed everything we owned, bought a house in Swan River, and moved there to take over running that practice. Our junior associate doctor in Stonewall bought our house there and became the primary doctor at that practice (she still works there).

The fight for control of our patients in Swan River was over before it really started. We were there seeing them months before our former doctor even managed to open her doors for the first time. Our revenues dipped a little the first year, but they came back and have been steadily growing ever since. The one casualty of our frantic move was my right shoulder. I had injured it back in 1993 but managed to get by pretty good for almost 20 years. The move finished it off though. I ended up with chronic pain and barely able to lift the arm after the move was completed. Cortisone shots and painkillers got me through to May of 2013 when the rotator cuff was surgically rebuilt. It is now relatively pain-free and is about 90% as good as it used to be.

We had barely moved when our daughter started experiencing weird cyclical fevers that nobody could explain. We finally ended up taking her to the Children's Hospital in Winnipeg where she was diagnosed with Systemic Juvenile Rheumatoid Arthritis just a few days before her 4th birthday.

This is a rare disease that only affects a few dozen children in Canada annually. In its worst incarnation, it can leave a child painfully crippled by their teens. However, when caught and treated early, it has a good rate of permanent remission. Thankfully, that appears to be what happened with our daughter…she was declared in remission by February of 2012, and the specialist's opinion is that the disease will not return.

Meanwhile, the bank continued to squeeze our practices and threaten to take our assets. I continued to fight them off, and to argue the fact that they had no cross-collateralization. It took me over a year to finally prove that they had no right to be hurting our other practices, but they still wouldn't refinance them or release them from special loans.

After over a year they sent one of their top guys from Calgary, and our so-called special loans account manager from Saskatoon, to meet with our partner and us. I kid you not, a few hours before we were scheduled to meet our partner emailed to say that he wasn't going to show. This helped to convince the bank that we weren't the problem, but we were still under attack from them.

A few weeks later I finally figured out why the bank thought they had all our practices on the hook for the one problem clinic and brought it to their attention. I won't waste your time with the details, but I finally proved my case to the bank. They suddenly wanted to cooperate with us, and we were assigned to a new special loans account manager!

We made one last ditch effort to have the partner take over the practice. We were willing to let him have it for $1 plus he'd assume the debt of that practice. We would walk away from the tens of thousands of dollars we'd poured into it over the years. Incredibly, he wanted us to take a portion of the debt AND pay him to take over the rest!

We advised the bank what he wanted, and they hatched the plan to put that practice into receivership and allow us to buy it back from the receivers. This was much quicker and cheaper than trying to sue the partner; the bank assured us it could be done for about $40,000. So, in October of 2012, that's what happened.

We bought the practice back from the bank with their financing (not without some additional drama as the now former partner sabotaged the computer systems and attempted to negotiate additional money for the backup files). You really can't make this stuff up! All was going well until the deal was set to close in February, and the bank informed is that the cost of the receivership was $100,000 more than they were expecting.

The senior guy from Calgary called me and said that the bank was prepared to absorb that $100,000 in additional fees, but that if they did, we would have no further help from them whatsoever. No new loans, not a single dollar of overdraft protection, nothing. He agreed to refinance our other practices finally and to give us an extra year on the loan to repurchase the problem practice if we'd accept responsibility for the $100,000. We accepted that condition.

They finally released us from special loans in the summer of 2013 (or at least claimed to; we didn't see any difference). The bank now had what

Ben Pritchett: Never Give Up!

they wanted, full cross-collateralization, and we paid all the costs. They gave me two years to turn around the problem practice. We had what we wanted, control of our businesses, and we were finally going to get properly financed again. Oh yes, we now had yet another account manager!

Yes, you probably guessed it. The bank stuck us with the extra $100,000 in fees but never gave us a single dollar of the promised refinancing. When I called the bigwig in Calgary to demand that he keep his word, he claimed not even to remember our account or what the deal had been. Make a note of this, a verbal commitment from a banker isn't worth the paper it's written on (since there is no paper in a verbal commitment, it's completely worthless).

This also reminds me of an old joke: "How do you know when a banker is lying to you? His lips are moving." Boy, did we experience that one!

We stuck our noses to the grindstone, and despite very limited capital, we began to turn the ship around. Then in January of 2014, the doctor at our other Winnipeg practice gave us 14 days notice and walked out the door.

Despite having been with us for years and discussing becoming a partner there, we later found out that she had spent a year planning her own practice, and even offered our key staff jobs to move with her (one of whom did).

This left us scrambling to find a doctor, which is tough to do in January, because the new grads start in August. We found one that didn't work out very well and decided to sell that practice.

By November of 2014, I had found a buyer for that second practice, and things were finally starting to go well at the original problem practice. We were, in fact, several months ahead of schedule to make that practice profitable.

We entered the Christmas season that year expecting 2015 to be a massive positive turning point for us. We had a buyer for one practice; the other

The Game Changer

was starting to perform nicely, our associate in Stonewall was ready to buy-in and become a partner. Things were coming up roses, after years of being on the ropes.

I projected that by the end of 2015 we'd own two and a half practices free and clear, and be virtually debt-free with the proceeds of the one sale and the partner buy-in taken into consideration. Barely two weeks into the New Year, disaster struck.

First, my Step-father died suddenly from a heart attack, and he was my severely disabled Mom's sole caregiver. Then only a day later, the bank called to inform me that they were calling all our loans, despite missing no payments and paying off nearly $2 million in the preceding 12 years!

I took care of the arrangements for my Step-dad. I had to have my Mom hospitalized as I simply couldn't take care of her and battle to save our companies too. (Good news there though, after being institutionalized for over 18 months, she's back home and functioning with my help and the help of home-care assistance.)

I shopped our business around to all the other major banks and alternative lenders with no success. They were all like a bunch of lemmings…over and over, I was told that our story was good, our numbers were good, but if the one bank didn't want us, then there must be something we weren't telling them. The concept that their fellow bank could be making an error never occurred to them.

So, we managed to sell the one Winnipeg practice as planned, and quite literally gave the other one away. We borrowed expensive private money from lenders to pay off smaller creditors and to keep the practices going while we sought other solutions, but there were none. Finally, in June of 2015, we declared bankruptcy.

With the stroke of a pen, we watched 12 years of hard work and a 7-figure net worth disappear because a big bank would not keep its word.

Ben Pritchett: Never Give Up!

The end.

No, not the end.

We were lucky enough to have some very, very good friends who borrowed and loaned us close to $250,000 to keep our Stonewall and Swan River practices going. We went bankrupt on a Friday and reopened on Monday with a new name, in the same old locations. It was totally seamless with most of our suppliers and our patients not even realizing anything had changed. Same for our staff in those clinics.

We bought back nearly all our assets from the accounting firm appointed by the bank to liquidate our assets and kept on trucking. Corporately, at least.

Personally, we were in bankruptcy for 21 months, and it was a constant struggle with the bankruptcy trustees. We obviously stopped making payments to the bank that had screwed us over, and we had no choice but to give up and stop paying our credit cards, but we kept paying everything else.

We were repeatedly told to stop paying our mortgages and private lenders because the debts could be wiped out with the bankruptcy, but we refused. These secured lenders had not caused the problem and should not be caused to take losses…and we did not want to give up our assets.

While bankrupt our practices actually grew, and we started a specialty Vision Therapy clinic as well. All are doing well.

My wife had wanted me to take a year off to recharge after we declared bankruptcy, and this lasted a total of 12 days! I got a call from the business coaching company I had been involved with for some time. I had explained what was going on and told them I'd have to take a couple of years to regroup, but they were having none of it and bent over backward to keep me involved.

We were released from bankruptcy the day before my 46th birthday in March of 2017. It was the best birthday that I've had for many years, and I'm certainly glad that I was around to celebrate it because I very nearly wasn't. Today, we still have some issues. The bankruptcy will be a black mark on our credit bureaus for 7 years.

Our friends who borrowed money to save our businesses are dealing with fickle private lenders (although, they can't be worse than the banks), until we finish paying them off. It will probably still be a few years before we can return to normal business banking and creditworthiness in the eyes of traditional lenders.

Staffing continues to be a nightmare for us (and every other employer) both in office staff and doctors, but we seem to have a great crew for the moment. The future is looking brighter.

One of the things that got me through the bankruptcy was the expectation that we would sue the bank when we were discharged, (you can't be sued or sue anybody while bankrupt). I had met a lawyer before the bankruptcy who thought we had a case and was even willing to take the case on contingency. However, post-bankruptcy I have decided that this bank has stolen enough of my life and any settlement is not worth the time and psychological toll that the lawsuit would take, even if there was no cost.

I've written an international bestselling book on business systems since the discharge. I have another book in the works, a course on business systems is planned, and I'm preparing to launch a mastermind for independent optometrists wanting to grow their practices and to stay independent. And a few other projects.

I'm an entrepreneur and will be one until I die. But, I wouldn't be here if my wife hadn't said, "I'd rather be poor with you, than wealthy without you." May you have somebody equally strong by your side for your battles …and if it's something worth fighting for, fight with everything you've got!

I started with a favourite Winston Churchill quote, I'd like to conclude with another: *"Never give in, never give in, never, never, never, never–in nothing, great or small, large or petty–never give in except to convictions of honour and good sense."*

ABOUT THE AUTHOR

BEN PRITCHETT was born and raised in Gander, Newfoundland, where he started his first business at the age of 15 and began his own consulting practice in 1991. For over 26 years he has worked with clients in dozens of different industries. Companies coached by Ben have nearly doubled and tripled their revenues in a single year.

He has taught business management at a private college, run optometry clinics, owned a business brokerage, a specialty computer company and a sales training business. While not everything was a raging success, he learned a lot about business—both good and bad—along the way. Ben says that, "when things come too easily, you really don't learn much, so appreciate tough times for their learning opportunities. Otherwise, your time and money were wasted."

Ben's a life-long learner with 3,000 books in his current collection). He tries to attend two to four National business events every year to keep up with what's working for other businesses, in other industries, all over the world, and believes that you're moving backward if you aren't constantly learning.

He's the author of "Systematize It Now!: The Art of Taking Back Your Life & Your Business Or Professional Practice–With Less Stress and More Profits!" It became an International Amazon Bestseller in 2017.

He's currently putting the finishing touches on a specialized mastermind program for optometrists but says that it can be used by any entrepreneur wanting to grow their business with less stress along the way. If you'd like to learn more, contact Ben via email at ben@advantagebizconsulting.com.

Ben Pritchett

(Be sure to ask him about an extra special offer on his 52-week marketing training program.)

Ben currently lives in Swan River, Manitoba, Canada, with his wife Dawn, daughter Calleigh, and two lovable Airedale Terriers named Darth Vader and Princess Leia (yes, he's a Star Wars fan too). Ben loves to work from home with his furry "assistants," and can often be found burning the midnight oil on some new project or another.

Despite an already hectic schedule, he takes on select consulting assignments when a project piques his interest and would welcome the opportunity to work with you if you have a business that you want to grow successfully.

The Game Changer

BRADY PATTERSON
Phoenix Rising

It was late October 2001, I woke up and looked around, confused where I was. I was on some sort of couch in what seemed to be someone's basement, but I didn't even know who's home I was in. Wincing from a headache, I sat up and tried to get my bearings, but no amount of looking around the dim space clued me in to where I had ended up. I thought back to last night, what had I done? Who was I with? What the hell happened?

All I did was go out for one drink with some friends, right? I had all these unanswered questions swimming in my mind and only small flashes of experiences. I remembered being at a pub, then flash to a bar, flash to hooter shots from my buddy's mom, flash to cocaine in the bathroom, and flash to smoking a joint outside, and no idea of the order these happened in.

Standing up slowly, I knew I had to go up the stairs and find out where I'd ended up this time.

This was my life. I blacked out nearly every time I drank, and every day felt the same as the last. Have you ever felt like you were just going through the motions? Maybe each day that preceded today felt the same and like this was an endless cycle? There's a theory in psychology about being a product of our environment. If that runs true, shifting our environment can make a difference in how we show up in the world.

For me, that environment was killing me softly, with my participation. By the time I reached high school, we lived what a lot of people would have considered an ideal life from the outside, but on the inside, I was a mess. Growing up we had moved a lot, and each move meant new faces, new places, new schools, and new problems. But to make this crystal clear, let me rewind way back, before I was conceived. If environment plays a part in shaping us, mine came into full swing well prior to being born. My parents had another boy before me; his name was Bradley. Due to some bullshit twist of fate, Bradley never made it out of the hospital and passed away shortly after birth. Two things happened at that point, one, my parents lost a child and two, I lost an older brother.

Having that happen, I'm sure you can understand that this affected my parents a lot. I ended up being born and was followed by a sister soon after that. Thankfully we were super healthy, yet the original loss had forever altered the future. My father, who was already an alcoholic, sunk even further into his pain. My mother, who guarded us fiercely, did so until she could take it no longer, and they separated. We moved, then moved, and then moved again. This became our life. Even when she was able to find a man to be with, that instability was always present, and the one she settled with was not a pleasant one. Currently, there is a report filed every 10 seconds regarding child abuse, and 80% of those followed up with exhibit psychological problems by the age of 21.

My environment was shaped by spankings, cuffs on the head, and constant belittling. All of this took place away from the eyes of everyone, even my mother. That changed later in life, but at first, it was very hidden. I learned to distrust people, especially people in authority. This wasn't the exception but the rule, but I did have one exception, and that was Neil, my Tae Kwon Do instructor. By this time, I had already discovered alcohol, drugs would come later and having him as a mentor for those few years before moving away again was a grounding force that kept me out of a lot of trouble. I

Brady Patterson: Phoenix Rising

still got in fights and did silly teenage boy things, but such is life.

By the time we moved to the last place I had lived with my family, I was a lost soul, but here, things changed. I went from being a shy, withdrawn, often-bullied person, to being one of the more popular kids in town. This new shift in the environment brought about a definite shift. Instead of hiding in books, work, or the woods, I could now hide in plain sight. I drifted like a chameleon through these final years of school. I did quickly settle into a group of outcasts, but never quite committing to any group of people, keeping my distance so no one could hurt me. I discovered drugs, escalating very quickly. Drugs, cutting, partying, booze, and more became my day-to-day. I was trying everything legal, or illegal in sight to help me stay hidden. I was seeking ultimate escape.

This is something you might know about. Having that drink or toke to take the edge off of a long day at work, playing video games endlessly with your internet friends so you can feel connected, or reading a book that keeps you so engaged you don't have to feel your own life. What about binge-watching Netflix to avoid the work that's piled up? You starting to follow the environment thing? At the end of the day, it's much easier to manage your surroundings than it is to manage your mind and your environment consists of the things that surround you, the places you visit, and the people you spend time with. That's what I've learned in my time on this earth.

By the time I left home, I'd developed a pretty severe drug habit. I wasn't the typical user that comes to mind for most because I was a functioning addict. I held on to a work ethic I developed growing up, and so at any given time I had up to four separate jobs to fuel my $50,000 a year habit until my breaking point, and I'll get to that soon. I started to realize the power that my environment had on me and made some shifts. Just before my 19th birthday, I abandoned my life to try something different.

I moved away from all my friends, to a place that although I had family nearby, I had little contact with them. Its one redeeming quality to me was the seemingly endless wilderness. The wilds were a place I never felt like I needed to be anything but myself. Despite my time in nature, I quickly slipped back into my old habits, just with new people. That "after work drink" was two or three beers at the pub on the way home, then another six-pack there and maybe a joint. I managed to move the harder substances to the weekend or to a time when I knew I could recover in time for work.

After just over another year of living this way, I had my first major low. If you have ever been so crippled by depression that you can't get out of bed, you'll understand what I'm describing. I had come home from a long night shift at an unfulfilling job, and was standing in the kitchen when I had to lay down. Not go find a couch or bed to rest on, but collapse on the floor. It was like someone went into my body and removed all ability to stand. Lying there I knew where my phone was, but I couldn't summon the energy to get to it. I knew something was very wrong with me at the time so I inched my way to the wall and managed to knock the phone out its cradle. I dialed the safest number I could think of, my mom's.

I have no idea what we talked about that day, but this was the day that I knew something had to change. I tried moving again to another city. I had a lull in my habits but soon picked up at almost the same pace as before. Within six months of my breakdown, I got fired for sleeping on the job, and I was moving again. This is where things went crazy. I moved in with my sister and started drinking a flat of beer a day, massive doses of psychedelics, and more.

You can see the trend here. Even with changing my environment, things weren't changing, but why? This is the question I was asking myself; Why is it that each time I move, things only change for a short time and then it's back to the normal routine. Why? As it turns out, each time I changed locations, I brought the same things with me, went to the same type of events, listened to the same type of music, had the same daily habits, and ate the same type of food. Few of which actively supported my life.

Consider then the habits and environment that support you? Are they

Brady Patterson: Phoenix Rising

working? Are you happy? Are you lit up from the inside? Do you wake up each day feeling supported and ready to play?

That wasn't true for me. My patterns were self-destructive, but they were about to make an abrupt shift. I had wrecked my motorcycle the previous year and decided to head home to Saskatchewan to see my family, and after a long bus ride, I arrived. That first night home I saw my family for a few minutes, and got a tour of my mom's new home. A short while later I asked my mom if I could borrow her car to visit an old friend. I planned to meet her, have a drink, then go home. If it weren't for this night, things would be much different for me. That night was my turning point. That was the catalyst to trigger me to quit smoking, drugs, and alcohol in one day, cold turkey. It wasn't an easy task, but I finally understood what impact my environment had on me.

You see, I have a younger brother, and my visit was near his birthday. He was out with friends during my visit, celebrating, and they had planned to come home to play video games until the wee hours but were confronted by an idiot, that was me. They had to change their plans that night, and I don't remember what they did instead if anything. When I came into the kitchen the following morning, my brother was looking at me with a look I'd never seen on his face before.

The first words I remember from him were, "who drove last night?" I mumbled something about, "keys please," and went to grab some coffee. "That's funny because when I got home last night mom's van was sideways across the driveway, drivers door open, still in gear, up against the neighbour's fence." I didn't know how to respond, but that explained the look. This young man who'd looked up to his older brother for many years was for the first time looking down, in a way that I could feel the disgust he felt. He took care of me though by parking the car and making sure to talk to me about it first. Growing up I had always tried to look out for him and keep him safe; now he returned the favour.

It was in that moment with my brother that I had a realization that forever altered my trajectory. I promised myself that I would never again see that look on his face towards me. I chose to rise. I went to work designing and making the shifts in my external and internal environment that I needed to make. I cleaned my immediate environment and got rid of all the drug paraphernalia, gave away the booze I had left, and looked for other things around me that weren't supportive.

I started to take courses and training that supported me being better and put me in touch with a community of people that supported my changes. I started hanging out with people that were doing something significant in the world and seeing changes as a result. I joined a men's group, hired a life coach, and, not long after, a business coach. All these were additions to my environment that overwhelmed the few unsupportive things I had left. It was a tipping point, and I was flowing with it. I had a fresh perspective, a new business, and within a few years, an amazing wife.

Oh, so on that morning when I woke up not knowing where I was, let me clarify. If it isn't clear yet, it was in my mom's new house. Those stairs I walked up to come face to face my brother was hers, and it was a very long walk. I still reflect on those days and the structure of my life at that point.

Without those experiences, I wouldn't be who I am. At the same time, I know that what and whom I surround myself with plays a key role in my life and I'm happy to have the architecture of life supporting me every day. Today because of my choices I live in one of the most beautiful places in the world and am married to the most wonderful woman. Life still throws the occasional curveball at me but thanks to the way I've crafted my life, I'm ready for it. Are you?

Brady Patterson

ABOUT THE AUTHOR

Like you, Lifestyle Architect and Survival Instructor BRADY PATTERSON has seen the word success defined numerous ways over the years. Is it financial? Is it a happy family? Is it all about the environment? Is it meant only for the chosen few? Or, is there more to it?

With over 15 years in business, 25+ years of wilderness time, men's work, running masterminds, he has most importantly, real-life, in-the-trenches experience and his view is radically different. Brady looks at the environment around you as the foundation of where you're at, and shares with listeners, that success is a moment-to-moment choice and is affected by the interaction between the internal and external forces. Success is for everyone, every day. It's how we should live our life.

Brady is sometimes referred to as the "Bear" for his ability to get directly to the point and is known for his practical style; Brady's fusion of the environment and the spirit connect with his clients at an intimate, intense and individual level.

Brady grew up on the farm, ran a successful DJ business, and spent more than a decade solving problems in the oilfields of Canada for companies like Husky, Shell, Nexen, and more.

Facebook: www.facebook.com/thebradypatterson
Phone: 778 689 2025; Consultation phone 604 535 0406
Twitter: @bradypatterson
Instagram: bradypatterson
Websites: www.bradypatterson.com | www.architectyourlife.com

The Game Changer

CHUCK SUTHERLAND
I discovered a huge secret that changed my life forever!

I was 30 years old, and I thought I was a failure!

I bought a hotel property from my best friend who had a large real estate investment company. My down-payment was $350,000 in property and cash. He provided a seller-financed, carry-back mortgage. The notes were pledged back to me for things he had to do in the future. I thought I had created a very smart deal as I also didn't have any payments to make for two years.

However, a year later, after I had invested another $75,000 in renovations, he declared bankruptcy. I then learned that the notes I had signed and that were returned to me as my security for contractual promises he made to me were also pledged for loans he had at three other banks. In case you are not following this, the bottom line is that he and his company had committed fraud against three banks…and me!

When his bankruptcy dust settled, I lost the property and was left with no money and no credit. I was terribly disheartened, but I had to carry on anyway.

The Game Changer

I started working as a real estate consultant, performing feasibility studies for real estate developers and investors. Fortunately, some people found me smart about real estate and hired me to do the studies for their lenders. The studies were frequently required by banks to approve (or disapprove) loans to real estate developers.

At first, I found the work interesting and challenging. But over time, I grew more and more frustrated by the pressures of both not enough money and not enough time.

To work, I needed to travel across the United States, wherever my clients sent me. I was gone about half of the time doing work for clients. The travel was physically demanding as I was on a plane at least twice a week, sometimes four times a week. I was tired!

I was also a single parent raising 4 of my 5 children. The constant travel and late-night work had me seeing my children less and less. I relied on my parents and one of my sisters to take care of my kids while I travelled.

For a while, it had worked. Then, it became harder and harder to make ends meet. Consulting projects were way down at one point, and I found myself frequently without any work at all. And if I didn't have any work, I also didn't have money. I was barely surviving financially.

One day, the electric company turned off the power to my house. I found myself exhausted and discouraged. I had worked my butt off for a decade, and I was getting nowhere. I couldn't even take care of my own family. I was angry at myself and my ex-wife.

I was sitting in the dark on the floor of my bedroom, suffering, crying, and blaming. I felt totally broken. "Why? Why? Why is this happening to me?" I asked that question over and over again!

Suddenly, sitting there in the dark, I had this massive realization that continues to change my life to this day!

Chuck Sutherland: The Secret That Changed My Life Forever

Despite appearances, I was actually living my life by myself. I had a business by myself. I was a single parent raising my four children…by myself. I was divorced which meant that I had no partner in life! I was by myself there, too!

I started thinking about what my father had taught me about partners. He had told me over-and-over for years, "Never have partners. They'll lie to you. They won't pull their own weight. Partners are not worth the aggravation."

I had followed my father's advice too literally. I didn't have any partners beyond my own family. Even with my family, there was no real partnership. They were just helping me.

I felt completely on my own!

When have you felt you were on your own, with no backup or support? I'll bet it was a feeling similar to mine.

I vowed to myself then and there that I wasn't going to live that way anymore. I started thinking about where I could find partners for increasing my business and income. I was afraid to call people and tell them that because I didn't want them to think any the less of me. I'm sure you can relate to not wanting people to judge you.

I finally mustered up the courage to get on the phone. I talked to several people about this insight. When I was sharing that I had been doing everything by myself, I often left them confused by what I was sharing. But the more I shared with others, the clearer I was about how I had gotten to this point in my life and how to create my personal and professional life in a new direction.

I made an appointment with one of the richest men I knew. I had done a number of research projects for him and his friends. I thought he might have some ideas for me. We sat for about an hour in his office talking about the real estate business, where I was, and where I wanted to go. Instead of pretending everything was okay, I shared my insight, my desire for partnership and my motivation for a better life for my family and me.

At the end of our meeting, he offered me a partnership in a new division he wanted to start. He wanted to buy self-storage projects that were in foreclosure and turn them around. He offered a small salary with promises of a percentage of every deal we did. I didn't hesitate. We shook hands and started our partnership. I didn't know all the details of how we would set it up, but I was "all in!" I trusted in our newly created partnership and knew we would work out the details later to be mutually beneficial.

From there, we bought existing properties and turned them around through renovation and training the staff in effective self-storage management. We started building new projects as well. After a time, I stopped having money problems. And, surprise, I found I didn't mind the travel as much if I was making money!

All we did, and all I have become since that partnership was formed, was because of that one decision to stop doing everything by myself. I let partners into my life. Not just the formal, legal kind of partners, but partners in every aspect of my life. I vowed to look for partners in everything.

I had created a partner in business. I created partners to help me build buildings. I upgraded my relationship with my parents, brothers, and sisters to being my real partners in raising my kids.

Seven years later, I was talking to a woman over the phone about a non-profit cause we both were working on together. She was a partner in doing good. Marilyn was in Washington, DC and I was working in St. Louis. We talked for two hours, first about our non-profit work and then about every subject under the sun. And I don't think I ever laughed so hard in all my life.

Chuck Sutherland: The Secret That Changed My Life Forever

That two-hour conversation led to more and more telephone calls, and our first date about a month later in St. Louis. Our fourth date was Thanksgiving with her parents and our fifth date was Christmas with 43 members of my entire family.

We were married before the end of the next year and Marilyn became my partner for life. We became real partners with our children and in our approach to grandkids as well.

After we got married, I left the real estate partnership to spend more time with Marilyn and develop projects "on my own!" I had forgotten about the principles of partnership in my business! And in those tough times, it was all my "partners" who helped me rediscover this magic elixir to life. Relationships and Partnership!

Did I have any failures after that? Absolutely! If you are doing anything worthwhile, you will have failures. Sometimes, I have failed really big!

Through those years and the years that followed, I developed a system for creating partnership and relationships with people. I saw the system as one anyone could use to systematically build a reliable and profitable business. I had begun the journey almost accidentally, but have continued to refine it to this day.

I began to see the wisdom of other real estate trainers that had come before me. The best real estate secret in the world was that "people are more important than property." From that one premise, a real estate transaction became about providing a sufficient quantity and quality of benefits that would meet the needs for each and every party to a transaction. And building quality relationships and partnership in a transaction was the catalyst that pulled it all together. That secret is what altered my life forever. And I feel privileged to carry that torch for the rest of the days I have to live on this earth.

About the Author

CHUCK SUTHERLAND is a real estate developer, consultant, and coach to individuals and investment groups concerning the acquisition and profitability of investment real estate. He is a commercial real estate investor, developer and course instructor is based in Dallas, Texas. In the real estate business since 1971, Chuck has been involved in the successful development of single and multi-family residential, commercial, retail, industrial, hospitality and mini-storage projects. As either an investor/developer or consultant, Mr. Sutherland has participated in the completion of over $200 million in real estate transactions.

Chuck also is a development consultant, conducting feasibility and market studies for industrial, commercial, hospitality, retail, self-storage, mobile home and housing properties throughout the United States. Since 1990, Chuck has participated in the development and construction of numerous self-storage projects, hotel developments, and build to suit projects for national tenants.

Chuck is a member of the Society of Exchange Counselors (www.secounselors.com). He is a Member and President of the National Council of Exchangors (www://ncexchangors.com) in 2017 and 2018. He teaches several real estate courses nationally and has been awarded Excellence in Education Awards from the Society of Exchange Counselors and the New York Commercial Association of Realtors. He also trains real estate investors and licensees in Profitable Real Estate DealMaking.

Reach him by email at Chuck@CreativeRealEstateNetwork.com

JAMIE SULLIVAN
A Gentle Way: Intuition & Business Unite

I was living on Canada's wild West Coast on Vancouver Island. I'll describe to you a day in the life on the Island. The smell of salty ocean air, infused with the sound of rushing water, the awe of salmon making their way upstream, massive trees reaching for the sky and, deer that calmly stare your way as they continue eating.

One day quite like this, I decided what I wanted to do with my life. By this time, I had had many adventures, been trained by great teachers (and humbled by them too), and felt a clear sense of my calling. I wanted to restore a sense of magic to the world. Sweet, loving, enchanting, soothe-the-soul-awake magic. I was great at making people feel wonder, hope, and clarity, and even better at inspiring their imaginations to restore their own sense of whatever magic was to them. My professional title was "Certified Clinical Hypnotherapist"–C.Ht for short.

I was 32 years young and had been working as a Hypnotherapist for a few years by then. As a "Ducks-in-a-row" Specialist, I enlisted myself in a year-long business program where I would have a panel of "successful" business mentors to guide me in manifesting my vision of what I wanted to do with my life.

The Game Changer

It was that time in the program where we were to take our ideas, plans, and projections to the panel of mentors for review. I confidently explained the business model I wanted to move ahead with. In short, without the decor I typically place on my words, I was going to make and sell hypnosis mp3s and online courses. The response? A unanimous, "That will never work." The advice I got was even better. "You are charismatic, confident and based on your reviews obviously skilled. Our advice to you is to build up your practice to full-time and, over the next three years, work at establishing the local clientele to sell your products to." I was dumbstruck. "But they are the successful ones," I thought. "How could I be so wrong?" "It seems simple enough to me; I'm so confused now."

Guess what I did. Eeek surely, you're already cringing at what's coming. I benched my business model and my business plan. So that you know - ignoring my own intuition and listening instead to a panel of "successful" brick and mortar entrepreneurs was a MISTAKE. A few short years later, online courses were everywhere, and cd's soon died out, making way for millions in profit to be made from selling apps and mp3s. I was clearly AHEAD of the curve - until I ignored my intuition.

Guess exactly what I did not want to do? You guessed it. I did not want to establish a full-time practice that for me seemed awfully similar to making myself a job. But with more work, because now I'd have extra taxes, expenses, logistics and at times the weight on my heart of listening to a sea of untold tragic stories. You'll be happy to know I have many, let's say, kinks. One, in particular, saved the day-I have authority issues. I tucked that vision away safe in my heart until I could gather enough evidence to trust that it was appropriate to follow MY true north.

Fast forward a few years, and there I was, in a practice I found deeply meaningful, but not satisfying, and quietly nurturing my vision…slowly, …like a turtle.

IMPORTANT NOTE: Move! Move at any pace you can to build your dream life. ANY action forward is action and deserves credit. Once I had finished the business program, I made a dream board for my vision of what I wanted to do when I was a grown-up. Even though I'd had my confidence pummeled about what was possible for me as an entrepreneur, I knew if I was yearning to express myself in business "that" way it's because it was possible. In the centre of my dream board was/is a picture of a big beautiful tree sprinkled with twinkle lights against the backdrop of night, and a white snowy ground.

On the image are the words "Rested Willow," my first business name. While I have you, I'll plant a seed for you about the power of the subconscious mind (I am after all a Hypnotist!). A few months after I decided what I wanted to do when I grew up, I took a long quiet walk by myself along the ocean asking this question in the backdrop ("backdrop"…key word) of my mind. "What is this company I desire to build?"

I walked romantically alongside the ebb and flow of the waves every now and again stopping to write words in the beach sand. Suddenly there I was, writing the words Rested Willow in the sand. I stood back half in a dreamy, relaxed trance and read what I wrote. "Wheedoa," I said aloud. "WTF?" I said under my breath.

As soon as I got home, I researched the etymology and symbology of the words rested and willow. The results opened my heart and secured my confidence back into its rightful place. For the next few years, that dream board and the words Rested Willow would ensure I stayed true to my vision, even if it was at a turtle's pace. Besides, even if I wanted to blast off my own way, it would take a while for me to untangle my own thoughts and desires from that of all the advice I had gotten over the years about business, and even more so about what was expected from me as a human.

One thing I know for sure is that it's better to take time planning in the beginning than to get stuck in something that makes you miserable you think you can't get out of.

The Game Changer

I started a mastermind. It was more of a transformation group really, a small group of women ready to level up their lives with style. No more rigid structures and accountability that is so prevalent in groups for achievers, but instead rather soft lines, with flow that could move organically and just enough structure to give participants the certainty to throw down and win big. I thought of all the time it took me to lift the fog from my eyes because of listening to the outside world more than I listened to my inner world. I wanted to help others avoid the wolves of life, and hop along straight to granny's to share in some metaphorical warm cookies (Little Red Robin Hood).

So, I made a bet with myself. Yes, myself. I like that. It's fun. If you can't hold yourself accountable maybe you haven't found the right game in the first place?? Just saying. So, I made myself a bet. This chapter I was embarking on in my business would have to be 100% intuitive. I know right-how fun! Any and all agreements before that moment in time (i.e., clinic work) were safe from the dare, but the group I was about lead was not. Oh, what a relief!

Basically, I got a slam-dunk. With one simple dare, I provided myself with enough evidence to drop the bullshit one way to success for everyone and light a seriously divine fire under my bottom while providing a unique and nourishing way for my participants to fly. These are the rules of the dare I entered into with myself:

- I was allowed to make a skeleton for the 12-month long program.
- Then a week before our group time (once a month) I could begin contemplating what the best tactic was for our group time considering where each of the members were.
- Then, the morning of, I would wake early grab a cuppa, and finalize the plan for the day.

How I even came upon this grand game in the first place was by creating a hypothesis of how one could create the most transformation with the most

Jamie Sullivan: A Gentle Way-Business and Intuition Unite

joy while remaining true to the very intention of the group, which was to create massive improvements in their lives in as holistic a way as possible. That meant the results would not be isolated to one area of life but, they would be woven throughout one's life in a way that overall the results would be better than any attempt at achieving one isolated goal. The whole would lift itself! The most important thing I did was to consider basic psychological principles about how to hold space for groups, and then add in my own wisdom and leave out any rule that seemed to interfere with the participant's joy and sense of trust in themselves.

Overall, there were many imperfections and learning curves, some nerves each time I let myself relax and trust my wisdom, and definitely some great lessons I picked up that I've applied to my business and my life moving forward. The way I look at it is that I set the stage for me to politely decline the feedback of others who think they can do me better than I can do me. I created a context where my fear and the outdated opinions of others would have to step aside. I knew I was right in my methods. I knew kindness, love, comfort and the magic of MY brain could drastically shift how much pleasure, relaxation, and ease I could have as a business owner, teacher and guide.

The results we got as a collective I can barely find words for. They are still transforming because we went ahead and trusted a natural model of transformation that mimics nature and builds momentum. I followed my intuition, I took a chance, and the rewards were great for not only myself for but the participants also. And all I did was listen to the way we all, in this mysterious universe, appear to transform-then shared that perspective with them so they could, by default of being alive, discover themselves. Life and our greatest satisfaction, it appears, unravels from there. I could not have gotten that genius purely using strategy from books, and leading only in ways I thought were acceptable. I had to trust what I didn't understand, or couldn't quite explain. Put simply - I trusted love.

For me personally, I have always been a bit of a force. No literally, I've been pushy. Odd, since I desire nothing more than to soften into the roar

The Game Changer

of a campfire or the melody of a lullaby, and yet-in my life it was typical always to be pushing myself. I'm, let's say, in the process of retiring that way of life.

I feel freer to leap into my next chapter when leaping feels fun, and meandering my way forward if gentle and sensual call. So it appears intuition and business, personal happiness and a sense of magic are all intertwined. And I'd like to keep it that way. Next time you have an inkling about how to move forward, and it just doesn't make sense or shakes you a little, I suggest investigating a little further. You may really be onto something great.

P.S. That one group also paid for my basic expenses for the entire year—and I LOVED it.

Jamie Sullivan: A Gentle Way-Business and Intuition Unite

ABOUT THE AUTHOR

In her search to understand happiness, love, and timelessness JAMIE SULLIVAN has studied birth, death, creativity, relationships, sustainability, forgiveness and the whole encyclopedia of emotions. After 15 years of committed exploration and over a decade as a Clinical Hypnotherapist Sullivan has deduced down her learning and experience into potent medicine for the human soul.

She's a colorful woman who is gentle, fiery, brave and kind. Jamie's the founder and owner of The Truffle Box. Her mission is to empower our sleepy spirits to embrace the magnificence of our nature.

Visit **www.thetrufflebox.com** for a gift of inspiration and loads of free help.

The Game Changer

JANAK MEHTA
An Immigrant's Journey to Freedom & Fortune

Dead end job with no growth potential and a previous lay-off was enough. I was sick and tired of being treated by major corporations like a disposable diaper, and I knew it was time to step out on my own. With only three months of severance pay, I decided it was time to create my own financial destiny and start my entrepreneurial journey.

Before I tell you about my entrepreneurial ventures, let me start with my first few years in the US.

I arrived in the States from India with a dream and a computer engineering degree in August 1999. I joined Carnegie Mellon University for Masters in Computer Science, Electrical Engineering, and a Business school. After graduating from the prestigious university, there were several jobs (17 to be exact) to choose from, and I chose the Research Scientist position in telecommunications with Bell Communications Research Lab working on third-generation wireless networks.

I loved wireless technologies, and hence it was typical to spend twelve hours a day, along with weekends, at the office. My goal was to pursue a Ph.D. with Columbia University due to an alliance with Bell Communications

The Game Changer

Research Lab so I could then start my own High-Tech Company. I guess you could say the entrepreneurial bug has always been in me.

I was the model employee, and I loved the awards and recognition that it got me. I was making six figures. I was on top of the world. I felt like I made it!!! What happened next was something I could not have planned for. The 9/11 attacks shocked the whole world. New York area and stock markets were hit hard, and so was my industry – telecommunications.

Suddenly I was thrown in the unemployment market with a million other people in my industry. I realized how corporate America works. When they need you, they roll out the red carpet and when they don't need you; you are out. I decided at that time that I will start my own company one day.

But I didn't have enough cash, credit, or courage, and started looking for a job. First, I thought it would be easy since I had 17 job offers in 2000! I did not realize that finding a job was going to be this hard. For six months, I searched within the telecommunications industry before changing my focus. I decided to go back to Pittsburgh and work with my professor on a research project while continuing my job search.

Finally, after 13 months, my job search brought me to the automotive capital of the world–Detroit. I was hired by the Ford Motor Company, in March 2003.

I found the love of my life online! It's the best thing happened to me. And after getting a job, I got married, and my wife and I would talk about what our futures would look like. We both came from very humble pasts and knew that we wanted to make it BIG in our life. We started learning about real estate investing and in March 2004 started our real estate investment business. We bought many training programs and joined local real estate investment groups and jumped in with both feet. Within the first eighteen months of our business, we bought and sold $2.4 Million worth of properties. My wife managed the business while I was at Ford.

Janak Mehta: An Immigrant's Journey to Freedom & Fortune

By March 2005 we joined a local real estate mentoring group and became "model mentees." We started helping our mentor and ended up partnering with him to build a real estate investment club and attracted a growing number of members. We had monthly events with well-known speakers who flew in to share their wisdom. When growing the real estate investment club, we used many online marketing strategies to bring in new customers. Within 18 months we took the club from 0 to 300 members. Unfortunately, the partnership did not last, and we branched off on our own.

We had started learning about Internet Marketing from various Internet Marketing experts, and we attended conferences and seminars to sock it all in. We started implementing those strategies and started getting results. One example: We had bought Matt Bacak's article marketing system on CD and started implementing his strategies and then tweaked his strategies to Press Releases. We started getting results in our own real estate business. We then attended Matt's Millionaire Internet Training (MIT) and when we shared with Matt what we are doing. He suggested we start our own PR Writing and Submission company.

That's how PR Easy was born, and I quit my job at Ford Motor company in 2007! PR Easy started with creating and submitting an online press release to get first-page search engine rankings for clients. We expanded our services to include content marketing and Search Engine Optimization, Search Engine Marketing, and Social Media Marketing. Our clients were small business owners who are looking to maximize their internet presence.

While we were growing our marketing company; in 2008, Real Estate Market crashed, and we had to let go of all 18 properties, ended the partnership, and filed for Bankruptcy in early 2009! It was the worst time of our life. We realized that we had stretched too thin and it was not a right partnership.

Looking back, it was a crash course in growing up in the entrepreneurial world. It was not easy, and I do not recommend this roller-coaster ride for the faint-hearted. I am glad that I have a wonderfully supportive wife who has stood by my side through the thick and thin!

While going through motions of being at a rock bottom; we had to re-invent ourselves. We focused on what we knew. Marketing & Hustling. We knew that Internet Marketing along with Social Media Marketing world is exciting and has huge potential. So, we started another division of our company called Social Media Michigan-one of the fastest growing social media training organizations in the Metro Detroit area.

We grew Social Media Michigan to over 500 members and each month we had 80–100 people attend our meetings. With that, we started coaching our members and started a local mastermind in Michigan. We streamlined our services and started focusing on Paid Advertising (Google) and organic Social Media Marketing management for our clients.

We got back on our feet and started growing again. This time we were a lot more strategic, and we had fun along the way. By 2014, we had decided that we are going to focus on just ONE THING. We asked ourselves a very important question; "Out of everything we do what are we really, really, really GOOD at? The answer was Social Media Marketing & Advertising and more importantly Facebook Advertising and Marketing. We had slowly moved away from training, coaching and other services and now we focus strictly on Paid Advertising (Facebook, Instagram, Google Adwords) and Social Media Marketing. We now help our clients generate new leads, sales and new clients, customers, or patients in their business.

After growing business and selling multi-million dollars' worth of information products, services and coaching we moved from Michigan to Scottsdale, AZ , and we are now looking to grow our business at even more rapid pace.

Here are some of the key lessons I have learned so far in my journey of being my own boss:

Janak Mehta: An Immigrant's Journey to Freedom & Fortune

1. Take great care of your Clients/Customers: Client/Customers are your biggest asset in any business. When you genuinely care of your clients and customers; your business will grow, and you will sleep better at night!

2. Make sure you have the right partners: I have had bitter experience in partnering, and I think one should be careful before deciding to form partnerships. If the other person is not that committed, then it is a matter of time before the partnership ends. One of the reasons my wife and I get along so well is that we bring complementary skills and hence that partnership has been invaluable in achieving our goals.

3. You are in a Marketing Business: Without marketing, there will be no sales hence no business. So always be in control of marketing for the business. You can outsource individual marketing tasks but make sure that you are in charge of marketing strategies for the business.

4. Invest in being mentored: Mentorship is very important to get the information and support from the right people who have already succeeded in your field. I do recommend that you become part of two types of mastermind groups. One group should be from within your industry and the other one from outside the industry. Cross-pollination of ideas is very useful in taking the business to the next level.

5. Invest in Personal Development: We have gone through a lot in life. My wife and I have invested (time, money and effort) in growing personally and professionally. We have worked on our relationships, mindset (80% success is responsible for having a right mindset) and skills. Entrepreneurship is a journey to become the best version of yourself.

I want to end this chapter with my gratitude towards my family, friend, and this country. I believe that you get second chances in very few places in this world and this is one of those places.

The Game Changer

So, if an immigrant with a dream and determination can make it in this country; you can too!

Never Give up and Make it Happen!!!

Janak Mehta: An Immigrant's Journey to Freedom & Fortune

ABOUT THE AUTHOR

JANAK MEHTA is known as a "Facebook Advertising Ninja" and is recognized "Paid Advertising Expert," serving clients worldwide.

Janak Mehta is the co-founder of Clients Online, a full-service Facebook Advertising Agency based in Scottsdale, Arizona. Clients Online helps e-Commerce Business Owners, Experts, Information Marketers, Influencers, Speakers, Authors, Coaches & Consultants grow their business with Facebook & Instagram Advertising & Paid Advertising Campaigns.

Clients Online has a unique Reverse Engineering ROI™ method to define key success goals and the Facebook Trifecta™ method to build, optimize and scale client's campaign.

Janak is a serial entrepreneur who started his career as a Research Scientist at Bell Communication Research Lab and then worked as a Business Analyst at Ford Motor Company. He co-founded PR Easy (Now Rebranded to Clients Online) a full-service Digital Marketing company in 2007 and quit his full-time job! He also co-founded Social Media Training company – Social Media Michigan in 2008.

If you want to leverage the power of Facebook Trifecta™ and Reverse Engineering ROI™ methods to drive traffic to your sales funnels, generate more qualified leads and grow your business, then you must schedule a FREE 30-Minute Strategy Call with the Facebook Advertising Ninja: ($500 Value)

The Game Changer

KRYS PAPPIUS
Surviving the Perfect Storm

It is 2003. Our society measures success by outward appearances and material possessions. Anyone looking in on my life will consider me successful. I am into my 9th year as a police officer, a stable and well-paying job. I own my home, I own my car, I have no debt, and my work schedule allows me to indulge my love of travel. Europe is my usual destination. It all looks so GOOD.

December 25, 2003, I report to work for a night shift. In the locker room, I put on my uniform, my ballistic vest and my gun, the essential tools of the trade that shield me from the very people I have sworn to serve and protect.

At 5 am, my shift and I respond to an "in progress call," one of those calls where we all drop what we are doing and head to the scene.

At 5:20 am, during the investigation, I come upon a suspicious vehicle and advise dispatch that I will be initiating a vehicle stop. The driver pulls over, and I get out of my car. I start walking towards the truck.

Suddenly there is a squeal of tires, and the driver takes off at a high rate of speed.

The Game Changer

I run back to my police car. I am multi-tasking: putting my car in drive, accelerating, closing the door, putting on my seatbelt, reaching for the radio.

At 5:22 am it is all over for me and what is left of my police vehicle is a crumpled mass of metal in the middle of the roadway.

What I was not aware of was that the bridge deck I drove onto was covered in black ice. I started fishtailing, hitting one side of the bridge deck, bouncing off, sliding across into the opposite lane, hitting the railing, bouncing off, side to side, gaining momentum with each hit, down the length of the bridge. My car came to a stop when it hit a concrete pillar at the far side of the bridge deck.

As this collision was unfolding, my life literally flashed before my eyes, and at that moment, I felt a great deal of sadness, sadness because I knew that if I did not survive this event, my life would have meant very little. I was not leaving any legacy of value. I had not made a difference.

But something else happened. I realized I had absolutely no control over how this event was going to end and rather that resist, I simply, undeniably, surrendered. I knew that the final outcome was not mine to decide. I sat back in my seat and chose to meet my destiny eyes wide open.

My injuries were significant–pulled muscles, severe bruising and, most importantly, a broken pelvis that went undiagnosed for three months. For three months, I hobbled around in excruciating pain while being told "there is nothing wrong with you, just some soft tissue bruising," all while being pressured to get back to work.

When I received the medical care, I needed, and my physical injuries started to heal, I found myself going into a very dark place mentally. This crash came on the heels of another work-related critical incident and, as a result, four months after the crash I was diagnosed with PTSD. It would be a total of 15 months before I was fit to go back to work. Yet, in spite of the injuries and, in spite of the long recovery process, I believe that this was the best thing that ever happened to me. Why? For two reasons.

Firstly, this experience was my wakeup call. This experience forced me to own the fact that I had been living a double life. On the outside, it all looked so good. But on the inside, it was quite different. On the inside, I felt empty and unfulfilled and, truth be told, I found my life to be very boring.

Secondly, in that moment of surrender, a door cracked open just a little bit. I could sense, for the first time, that I was not alone, that there was an energy far greater than me, that surrounded me at that moment and that I could trust to do right by me. The door opened just a crack, but it had opened, for the first time.

After the accident, as I recovered physically, I also worked with a counsellor to deal with the symptoms of PTSD. It was a long haul both physically and emotionally.

In early 2005 I still felt angry, sad, and anxious. But physically I was functional again.

In March 2005, four Canadian police officers were murdered on duty. I attended their funeral, an experience I will never forget. Where else are funeral attendees protected by snipers on rooftops and helicopters flying overhead? You see, there was 10,000 law enforcement personnel at that funeral, and we were, basically, sitting ducks. It was a surreal experience.

However, being part of that event, being part of something so much bigger than me, led me to conclude that the only way I could honor the four downed officers was to go back to work and do the best job I could. Looking back, it was perhaps not the best decision, but that is the benefit of hindsight.

Soon I was back into my routine. But something was different. I could not shake the feeling that there had to be more to life than what I was experiencing yet I struggled with what that could mean.

I am very curious by nature and started reading voraciously, trying to find an answer. Something was missing, and I had to figure it out. I started reading every self-help book I could get my hands on. Wayne Dyer, Debbie Ford, Eckhart Tolle…I read them all. And while I found many of these authors inspiring, the reality was that once the book was read and back on the shelf, nothing in my life had changed. These authors could inspire me to dream of a different life, yet none of them offered a follow through, none of them told me how to implement change.

And then I opened Gary Zukav's "Seat of the Soul." I could not put it down. Due to my early experiences, "religion" had no place in my life. In plain English, Zukav helped me distinguish between "soul" and "religion," and in doing so, he offered me an explanation for the energy I had felt surrounding me during my crash. Although the anger, the sadness, and the anxiety persisted, I felt I had taken a small step forward. I started feeling hope, hope that perhaps there actually was something of value within me.

The next piece of the puzzle appeared in the work of Martin Seligman, the father of Positive Psychology. In particular, I came across these words:

"Curing the negatives does not produce positives…the skills of becoming happy turn out to be almost entirely different form the skills of not being sad, not being angry, not being anxious."

This was the first time I had heard that happiness was a skill. I was determined to learn this skill and, as a type A personality; I was determined to learn it on my own. Again, lots of reading and learning, and yet again, nothing in my life was changing. I had to find a new strategy.

In 2013, ten years after my crash, I met a woman who helped me change my life. This woman spoke with a heavy southern drawl and, at first, I struggled to understand her. But once I got used to the accent, I realized that she had a gift to share with me. The gift she gave me was the key to creating a life of meaning. It was so simple. The key to a meaningful life turned out to be the answer to 3 simple questions.

The first question is "what are your values?" I had to be clear about what qualities are "must haves" in my life, the qualities that must be reflected in my thoughts and my actions and my environment, for me to feel satisfied and complete.

This should be so simple, and yet I had no clue as to what the answer might be. Early on I learned that the world was a dangerous place. Physical assaults as a child left me feeling anxious and fearful. I was always *afraid*. I learned early in life that the only way to be safe was to be invisible, to melt into the crowd. Who I was at any given time was determined by who those around me wanted me to be. The only thing that was ever really important to me was to feel safe and to do whatever it took to be safe. That is all I ever cared about.

With time, I discovered that my top values are: empowerment, freedom, community, and beauty. Empowerment to effect change in my life, freedom to think, feel, and be who I want to be at any given time. A community of like-minded people who share my sense of adventure and curiosity and concern for those with whom we share this planet. And, finally, time in the beauty that is the nature that surrounds me. The life that I had been living before 2013 had, for the most part, reflected none of these values, these "must haves," and so my life was unfulfilling and boring.

The second question I had to answer was, "what are your beliefs?" Our beliefs are the lens through which we see the world around us. I had to examine the lens through which I saw the world, understand the beliefs that dictated the choices I made, and I needed to challenge any of my beliefs that kept me playing small, kept me trying to stay invisible.

I was a curious kid. My favorite question was "why?" I wanted to learn new things; I wanted to understand how things worked. At the same time, I had a very difficult time in school. I had trouble assimilating and retaining information. I remember undergoing a psych evaluation, and I remember being told that there was nothing wrong with me, I was just lazy. I bought into that judgment.

Add to that, is the fact that I was in a school surrounded by nuns who told us every day, "in my country we do not speak to idiots." Those nuns drummed into us a religion in which God was a vengeful all-knowing being who would send us to hell for eternity if we were not perfect. The result is that I had a deep-seated belief that I was a lazy idiot who would burn in hell because I could never be perfect.

As a young adult, a sexual assault added another layer of fear and another layer to my sense of self that was both twisted and painful.

At the time, I sewed my own clothes. I remember the day I finished a cute little polka dot dress. It was flowing and had frilly little sleeves, and I felt like Marilyn Monroe wearing it. The first day I wore that dress was a beautiful, sunny day. I felt feminine and gorgeous! I was heading into town for lunch and had to take the subway. What started off as a joyful day ended with me being sexually assaulted by a stranger.

The impact that had on my sense of self and my sense of security was devastating. I felt shame; I felt that I had brought this on myself because I had allowed myself to be visible. I believed I was damaged goods, which no one would ever want me. More importantly, from then on, I could never respect anyone who could not see the "true" me. I could not respect anyone that I could fool into believing I might be someone they would want to spend time with and get to know. I became a very lonely lazy idiot who would burn in hell because I could never be perfect.

By looking inward, by examining my beliefs, I was able to identify the gremlins that kept whispering in my ear that I was useless, stupid, damaged goods and that nothing good would come to me because I was a sinner. Although a few of these gremlins still rear their ugly little heads now and then, I now have the skills to shut them down so that their impact on my life is limited. I now know that I am creative, resourceful, and whole, that it is up to me to make the most of this life I have been given, and that I am just as able as anyone else to do just that.

I mentioned earlier that as my accident unfolded, a door had opened a crack, allowing me to feel surrounded by an energy that would do right by me. As I peeled away the layers of beliefs that had imprisoned me in a lonely and small life, a very unexpected healing took place: I reconnected with what I choose to call "spirit."

From early in life I have had the belief that I was not good enough, that I did not belong, that I was not worthy, that I was not lovable. I was sad, and I was lonely. But something in me always yearned to be seen and accepted. I now know that the part of me that kept saying, "Here I am, please just *see* me," was my soul, that non-physical part of me that is the repository of everything that is good and gentle and loving in me. Early on I rejected religion but unfortunately, I threw the baby out with the bathwater. I did not realize that "religion" and "spirit" were two very different things.

When I rejected religion, I also rejected spirit, not just the concept, but *my* spirit. I now know that, for me, re-connecting with spirit was a natural progression from the work I was doing to create a life that was meaningful. By peeling away the layers of self-destructive beliefs and re-connecting with the best in me, I also reconnected with spirit, the loving energy that, I believe, connects us all. It gave me the safety I needed to allow myself to be *me*, instead of who I thought people wanted me to be. It started me believing that I was *good enough*.

The third question I had to answer was "what is your purpose?" I had heard a lot of talk about "purpose," but for the most part, the discussion was around the purpose of life. That is too heady a concept for me. This question focuses on my purpose: What did I want to accomplish in *my* life? What did I want my legacy to be? I needed to find a purpose that was in alignment with my values.

The Game Changer

I became a police officer because, in spite of everything, I always knew I wanted to do something of value in this life. I believed that wearing a uniform would allow me to blend into something bigger than me. I would not have to stand out in a crowd. I would be part of a team that would work together to disempower those who hurt others. I could be the good guy, the hero so to speak, while at the same time melting into the background, remaining invisible.

Three weeks into training I became consumed with panic. I realized that something was wrong, but I could not put my finger on it. Looking back, I now understand that I had "imposter syndrome." I had fooled "them" into believing I could do the job although deep down I believed that I was a lazy idiot who would burn in hell because I could never be perfect. I felt unsafe and under attack because I knew that at any moment the truth would be exposed! Every day I felt like I had been run over by an emotional steamroller. But I stayed because, frankly, there was something familiar about this scenario, about feeling the outsider, about feeling like I was an imposter.

Looking back at it all now, 20 years later, it is clear that I had walked into a perfect storm, one in which I would have to fight for survival, one in which survival was not guaranteed. By 2013, I felt dead inside, living on auto-pilot.

The work I did to answer these questions brought me clarity and understanding. My values are empowerment, freedom, community, and peace. As a police officer focusing on offenders, that was not my mandate. My mandate was to preserve peace, protect life and property, prevent crime, enforce the law and apprehend offenders.

None of that has anything to do with empowering people to be the best version of themselves, and *that* is a purpose that brings meaning to my life. It does not mean one is right and one is wrong, it simply means that there was a disconnect between my soul's desire and the job I agreed to do. And that disconnect was significant enough that with each year that passed, I

Krys Pappius: Surviving the Perfect Storm

felt I had died a little more, until I felt like a walking dead.

Although the learning that I did in 2013 was simple, it certainly was not easy. I had to allow myself to be vulnerable, open to new ideas and it required faith on my part. Looking back, I cannot say what it was about my mentor, or about me, or maybe even about us together, that allowed me to feel safe enough to take this leap of faith. But I did, and in return, I have found faith, faith that the universe has my back, faith that I have a soul that is perfect just the way it is, warts and all. Faith that I *can* have a life that is rich, fulfilling and complete.

I am now clear about my values. I also know when I am being led by limiting beliefs and I have the skills to shut them down. What is left is creating a life of meaning. For me, that means sharing what I have learned with others. Our world is full of suffering and injustice. I cannot do much about the world at large, but I can focus my attention on those who truly are in my sphere of influence and who also feel like they are stuck without knowing why and without knowing how to get unstuck.

To them, I extend a hand and an invitation to learn from my experiences, to make changes from the inside out, to live their life in a way so that when it does eventually flash before their eyes, it will be a movie they want to see.

My awakening took ten years because my journey was anything but a straight line. I took many wrong turns but, more importantly, as a friend of mine loves to say, "you can't see the picture when you are in the frame." Since the problem was rooted in my thinking, in my beliefs, I could not see the problem until someone was able to mirror them back to me.

I now know that it boils down to just three questions: my values, my beliefs, and my purpose.

My purpose is now clear: my purpose is to help others find fulfillment by finding the answer to those questions for themselves, without taking ten years to do so. That is how I can make a difference. That will be my legacy.

ABOUT THE AUTHOR

KRYS PAPPIUS is a Lifestyle Design Coach and Transformation Catalyst. She is certified by the Coaches Training Institute of California (CPCC).

In 2003, Krys was living what many would call "a good life." She was in her 9th year of a career as a police officer, a stable, well-paying job, she owned her home and car, she had no debt, and she was an avid traveler.

A serious car crash that year was a wakeup-call for Krys. It forced her to acknowledge while she had all the trappings of success, her life was unfulfilling and boring. This realization triggered a journey during which Krys tried, on her own, to transform her life into one of meaning and purpose.

In 2013, ten years after her journey began, Krys found the key to transformation. For Krys, the key lies in answering three simple questions. Once she found herself on the right path, the changes in Krys' life were swift.

Krys' passion is to share what she has learned with success-driven women who find fulfillment elusive. Krys helps her clients to use their answers to her 3 questions to design the life of their dreams. She then helps them implement the changes they need to make, from the inside out, to transform their lives from "ho-hum" to "hell yes!" Krys lives in Abbotsford, BC, Canada.

To learn more about Krys visit her website at www.kryspappius.com.

LINDA A OLSON
An Entrepreneurial Dream

At ten years of age, I wanted to be an entrepreneur. I believed if I could help people get what they need, they would pay me for it. One day I had an idea. I purchased garden seeds, and on a Saturday afternoon, hopped on my bike and went from farm to farm selling my seeds. Everyone bought from me. It wasn't hard. It was the beginning of an entrepreneurial dream.

However, four years later, my dream came to a crashing halt.

Mom, standing in the entryway of our 1959 farmhouse, her breakfast apron speckled with bread crumbs from making our sandwiches, waved as we boarded the bus. "Don't forget! As soon as you come home from school, change your clothes and help with the potatoes." Her shouts barely reached our ears before the bus door unfolded to close out the crisp morning chill. Violet, Leonard, Vera, and I hurriedly settled onto the green vinyl bench seats just moments before the gas engine lurched us forward.

The fall harvest was in full swing.

Our family of seven knew firsthand, "if you don't work, you don't eat," and we didn't complain. Cracking open a steaming baked potato in the dead of winter was reward enough for our labors. Nodding my head briefly to Mom through the bus window, I settled into my own world for the hour-long ride.

The Game Changer

After the day's lessons and the long ride home, I hopped down the steps of the bus and lugged my book bag to my bedroom. I changed clothes—work in the garden required well-worn denim jeans and a hand-me-down loose, long-sleeved cotton shirt—and stopped in the kitchen to quickly make a peanut-butter-and-jelly sandwich. Tossing the dirty knife into the dishpan, I hurried to the garden to join the others.

Over one hundred sixty acres surrounded our three-bedroom farmhouse. We must have looked like a bulls-eye from the air, with our property being surrounded by towering trees, cultivated fields, a country road and our good-sized vegetable garden. Taking a bite of my sandwich, I pushed open the front screen door with my foot and saw that Mom had recruited some extra help for the day's task.

Grandma and Grandpa Warkentin along with Aunt Laurie nodded their friendly greetings. Three-year-old Karen, Aunt Laurie's older daughter, played with my little brother. Billy was two years old and melted everyone's heart with his bib overalls, bare feet, and winsome smile. He tagged along everywhere, always wanting to be part of the action. Today that action would include burrowing beneath the wilted potato leaves in our Manitoban soil to dig out the Red Russet and Golden Yukon potatoes which would be stored in the basement for the winter.

Mom looked out across the front field, her hand shielding her eyes from the late afternoon sun. She spoke quietly, within earshot of Grandpa. "Last year we took so many trips with the pails; today we'll use the front-loader to bring the potatoes right up to the front step, as close as we can get to the house."

Grandpa nodded, and Mom glanced my way. My ears had perked up at the overheard suggestion, and I was mutely anticipating her next words. Remembering how my arms had ached last year after hauling two five-gallon pails full of potatoes for hours, I would dearly love to avoid the myriad trips from the garden to the basement in the late-September heat.

"Would you like to drive, Linda?"

Linda A. Olson: An Entrepreneurial Dream

I broke into a smile. At only fourteen, I was already an old hand at driving the Cockshutt 35 tractor. Taking a turn driving large farm equipment was a common responsibility for most teenagers in the area, bridging the gap between childhood chores and essential farming tasks on the family homestead.

Mom continued her instructions. "We'll pile the potatoes in the front-end loader. When it's full, Linda, drive it to the front of the house. Then we'll unload it with the pails and carry the potatoes to the basement."

I nodded my obedience, and quickly ran to climb the thirty-four-inch tire, boosting myself into the red metal seat. I could already taste the dust flying in the autumn air, envisioning the tractor bouncing its way along the well-worn path to the house.

I parked the tractor near the garden where I joined Grandpa, Mom, Violet, and Vera. We emptied pail after pail of potatoes into the bucket of the front-end loader until it could hold no more without spilling. Now it was time to head back to the house. Hopping once again into the metal seat, I positioned myself behind the wheel and turned the key. I peered over the top of the faded yellow tractor and, carefully shifting into reverse, backed the vehicle away from the garden, turning the steering wheel to change directions. Next, I shifted into drive and steered the 5,000-pound tractor toward the doorway of our pink stucco farmhouse. Billy and Karen played on the front step, watching my approach.

I neared the house and released the hand throttle, one foot on the clutch and the other on the brake. This was so much easier than toting heavy pails, I thought. We'll be finished in no time. I pressed the brake, anticipating the deceleration of the Cockshutt.

It didn't happen.

The tractor didn't slow, didn't obey my command to slow its pace.

The Game Changer

I gripped the steering wheel for leverage and pressed harder on the brake. The huge machine refused to slow. Alarmed, I realized the house was rushing up too quickly. I gathered all my strength, slid off the seat to a standing position and, with all my weight, jammed my foot on the brake, pumping up and down, up and down, demanding that the wheels stop their turning.

No response.

Bewildered and confused, I sensed the betrayal of the machine beneath me, rejecting my efforts to bring it under control. Quickly it was swallowing the distance to the house. I locked eyes with Mom, silently pleading for split-second direction; all I saw was my own panic reflected in her eyes. I screamed the only explanation I knew.

"I can't stop the tractor!"

I kept jumping on the brake. The tractor aimed for the house as if it was an arrow headed for its mark. I stomped on the brake, the clutch, and then the brake again.

Nothing. I turned my head slightly to catch any sound of Mom telling me what to do, but all I could hear was the engine growling its refusal to halt.

I could see that Mom was screaming now, but I couldn't make out her words. I put all my weight on the steering wheel and lifted myself up slightly and came down hard on the brake with all the force I could muster. Oh, God, what do I do? The house is close—too close. I can't stop the tractor, Mom! I can't stop…!

Mom shrieked as the front-end loader slammed into the stucco wall of the house and white wooden doorframe. The impact threw me forward into the steering wheel. I straightened my body and heard the horrific sounds of splitting wood as the doorframe dismantled. But, the kids! Where were the kids? Where was Billy?

The tractor had slammed into the house exactly where Karen and Billy stood.

Linda A. Olson: An Entrepreneurial Dream

Billy, attempting to escape the huge machine that was barreling toward him, had taken one step in front of the stucco house, almost as if to mark his destiny.

The machine, its angry rumble still spitting fury, had halted its impulsive rampage just inside the double door. Through the swirling fury, I saw Karen's colorful floral blouse wedged between the splintered panels. Quiet whimpering told me she was alive—thank God! —and I strained to hear Billy's little-boy sobs.

My eyes swept the scene wildly, looking for the baby brother who giggled and chased fireflies. My heart cried the words my lips could not form. Where was Billy?

Mom, in three steps, sprang toward me and vaulted up the Cockshutt. Landing beside me, she jerked the gearshift into reverse and forced the family-friend-turned-enemy to back away from its prey. Then she yanked the key and killed the engine of the mad beast. We leaped off its back simultaneously and, seeing what we didn't want to see, ran to the crumpled overall-clad form on the concrete step.

Billy.

My brain shifted into autopilot. Get Billy. Get Billy!

I ran to the limp figure that only moments before had been playing with a bug on the porch with Karen. Grandpa frantically threw the broken boards of the front door behind them as Aunt Laurie grabbed little Karen. Out of the corner of my eye, I saw Mom hurdle the rubble to what had been the entry to the house. A moment later she leapt over the shattered doorframe—now empty of sheltering Karen—and bolted to the silver-grey Ford sedan parked in the garage, car keys in hand.

Scooping up Billy, I wrapped one arm under, one arm over the too-still shoulders, the same way I had held him as a newborn. His semi-conscious form molded easily into my body as I spun around with him to race after Mom to the

The Game Changer

car. Vera was close behind.

Even as I cradled his semi-conscious form in one arm and grabbed the door handle of the Ford with the other, I could not comprehend his injuries. Accidents were common in farming communities, and I knew that in the midst of an emergency, hands moved while hearts prayed. But now my head also pounded with slicing questions. Why wouldn't the tractor stop? Did I do something wrong? Why didn't I turn the wheel harder? Why did this happen? Billy isn't really hurt badly, is he? Why didn't the tractor stop?

That night we cried ourselves to sleep as reality set in. We had lost this precious little boy.

The very next morning, my Dad came to my bedroom door and said, "You've got to get up. We have to keep going." Getting out of bed was the toughest thing I did that day, the next day, and for weeks, months and years to come. You see getting out of bed meant facing my fear, guilt, anger, sadness, and loneliness… and as you know, that doesn't happen overnight. It was the beginning of a long journey, but eventually, healing came, complete healing.

Excerpt from *"His Ways Are Higher, One Woman's Journey of Self-Forgiveness Against Unbeatable Odds"* Amazon #1 Bestseller.

Years later as I reflected on my Dad's words, *"You've got to get up, we've got to keep going."* I felt like, symbolically, he had handed me a torch of courage and strength. Courage to get out of bed and strength to face whatever lay ahead. It was then that I recognized a simple pattern in dealing with my emotional pain.

    1. First, I had to identify and name the emotional pain that had surfaced. Was it fear, anger, loneliness, or something else?

    2. Then I had to decide to face the pain. It had to be a conscious choice.

Linda A. Olson: An Entrepreneurial Dream

3. Thirdly, I needed to take action. Just because I had decided to address the pain, didn't mean I took action on it.

With one foot in front of the other, I somehow gathered enough courage and strength to face the daily challenges and eventually rose above the emotional pain. Addressing the daily challenges opened up the pathway to deal with the bigger pain that was buried was deep.

Fifteen years after the accident I had been accepted to graduate school in Southern California for a Marriage & Family Therapy program. The program required each student to take at least 25 hours of personal therapy and 25 hours of group therapy. I really thought I was doing quite well so decided I would get the personal therapy hours out of the way as soon as I could. After waiting two months for a highly sought-after therapist, I began my therapy. In the first session, she quickly identified the guilt that was buried so deeply… and said, "We'll deal with this when you are ready."

Two months later, I faced one of the most difficult days of my life as she walked me through in slow motion the worst day of my life – the day we lost little Billy. I sobbed from such depths I didn't know if I would ever recover. My therapist didn't want me to drive home in this emotional state so had me wait in another room.

As I calmed down, I experienced something I had never experienced before. I heard a voice in my head, as clear as could be, that triggered a brief conversation. "Has God forgiven you?" I responded, "Yes." "Do you believe your parents have forgiven you?" "Yes" Then what keeps you from forgiving yourself?" I didn't have an answer. The voice went on, "Are you bigger than God?" "No, I'm not bigger than God." "Then, can you trust God to help you forgive yourself?" With that, I got on my knees, and with God as my witness, I begged, "God, please help me forgive myself for the accident with little Billy." As I stood up, I experienced unbelievable freedom. The huge load of guilt was lifted.

As I reflected on that extremely tough day of my life, I recognized that deeper healing comes when our heart is ready and open. It is a process.

As long as we are willing to get help and deal with what we know we have to address, it will open up the way to get to the core. The best part is that getting to the core is like finding the gold, the true character and wealth of our story.

The deeper healing in my life brought a whole new perspective. I had risen above my self-limiting beliefs, and I could dream again. My entrepreneurial dream had not died. It had just taken a big detour to build the character I needed to fulfill my BIG DREAM. And better yet, with the help of my coach I was able to tell my story with the power it is worth. I had finally owned my story.

Through one of my dark days, my cousin said, "The sun will shine again for you some day." At the time, I could not even comprehend that may be possible. Now, I enjoy sunshine nearly every day. I am so grateful for the healing in my life. Without friends, family, co-workers and the help of professionals, I would not be who I am today. But even more than that it is my personal faith in Jesus Christ that carried me through the dark times and ushered me into the sunshine.

As I came to complete healing, I knew more than anything I wanted to help others discover and share their story. If I had a story, so did everyone around me. Out of my passion to reach more people and help them believe they have an important story that matters, I began scripting, *"Your Story Matters! 3 Breakthrough Secrets to Stories That Transform."*

In the last 40 years, I've helped thousands of people with recognizing they have a story. For some, I have had the opportunity to help them find their story, for others I helped them find healing in their story and still others I have shown them how they could use their story to attract potential leads to their business.

My new mission is to "Impact a million people a year through story," and

Linda A. Olson: An Entrepreneurial Dream

thus my entrepreneurial dream gave birth to *"Wealth Through Stories,"* a program that empowers entrepreneurs, speakers, authors, coaches, and leaders to share their story wherever they go. For more, I invite you to take a peek at my website **www.wealththroughstories.com**.

If there is one thing I would like to leave with you, please know you have an important story that others need to hear.

ABOUT THE AUTHOR

LINDA OLSON, Founder of Wealth Through Stories is an International Speaker, Story Expert, and Amazon #1 Bestseller. Her mission is to impact a million people a year as she trains entrepreneurs, speakers & leaders to find and share the wealth in their story.

Linda resides in Southern California with her husband, Rick, two beautiful daughters, handsome son-in-law's and adorable grandchildren who are the best part of her story.

For more, go to **www.wealththroughstories.com** and **www.wtssytem.com**

LISE LAVIGNE
50 Shades of Wrong

I am sharing this part of my secret life to the world because I know there are innumerable women in the same or similar situation I found myself in. There is a way out, and you can change your life.

Let me tell you about my own Christian Grey. It was love at second sight for me. When he picked me up at my doorstep wearing his Armani suit and black Italian shoes, I thought to myself this is the man of my dreams. He had the look I wanted, and I could see myself spend the rest of my life with him. He was tall, dark and extremely handsome. His sparkling eyes were so captivating I would get lost in them. When he smiled, I would just melt like ice cream on a warm day.

On our first dinner date, we went to a fabulous fine dining restaurant, a six-course meal, and had champagne. He said all the right things and the sexual energy between us was very intense. He was my dream man. He was certainly lots of women's dream man; I noticed how other women looked at him. He was sexy, gentle, yet strong and very romantic. His walk was confident, and he had a swagger about him that exudes sexuality. He was a well-respected businessman and very wealthy.

Being with my Christian Grey was always exciting and wonderful. We went to the best restaurants, the best places, and he truly knew how to

The Game Changer

make me feel like a lady. He was giving me nothing but the best. I thanked God for him because after all, I met this man through a personal ad I placed on the internet. How fortunate was I to have found him? We had a great lifestyle. He had all the expensive toys: the fancy cars, the fabulous house, and the yacht. We enjoyed fine wines, fine dining, weekend getaways and everything else that money can buy.

It felt so right being with him and when we were apart a piece of me was missing, even though we talked several times a day on the phone, I longed to be with him. Being with him was all I could think about. His presence was all I wanted because when I was with him, I felt whole again. He was like a drug to me, and I needed to be with him. We saw each other a few days mostly on weekends. Every weekend was fantastic, and we had the best times together.

Our sex life was very exciting, and somehow it got better and better each time. I felt so close to him. He would also tell me that I was the best he'd ever had and that he's never felt so loved by any other woman before. We talked about our future and that we would always be together.

This relationship was so important to me because it felt so good. I felt like finally, Cinderella had found her Prince Charming and that Cinderella will live happily ever after. It was a dream come true. I loved him so much that I would do anything to make him happy. I made sure I looked great all the time. I went out and bought new clothes that I knew he would like. I spent money on manicures and pedicures regularly. I bought tons of sexy lingerie and shoes to get him turned on. I did everything in my power to please him and keep him interested.

At a young age, I learned that to make people happy I had to do whatever it takes to please them. I always thought that to get love; I had to do things I didn't want to do. I had been doing that all my life and of course in my romantic relationships I held nothing back. I grew up to believe that sacrificing my own happiness for others is the best sign of loving someone.

In my relationship with my darling Christian Grey, it was no different. I gave him everything I had because I knew he was the one. What we had was very special. I had found the man of my dreams, and I was going to do anything to make him happy. One night he asked me if I watch porn, and I replied that no I hadn't watched porn. He then suggested that we watch it together.

When he asked me this, I felt like someone punched me in the stomach. I had this pain in my gut, and I felt very uncomfortable. Then I started to rationalize in my mind. "Well the experts say that porn is actually good for couples and relationships. I mean everybody watches porn, don't they? It's a billion-dollar industry so it can't be that bad." The sharper the pain my gut became, the harder I was rationalizing. After a while, the pain subsided, and I accepted to watch porn with my dream man.

It wasn't something I was enjoying at all, but like a good girl, I was making my man happy. What's better than making the man you love happy? Watching porn became a regular thing for us after a while and the more we watched it, the more I became desensitized to it. The only thing that mattered to me was that he was turned on and thought I was the best girlfriend ever. What happens when you watch more and more violence? You become accustomed to it, and it doesn't shock you anymore. It becomes normal, and it's no big deal. That was my experience with porn. I equate it to the gateway of a slippery slope into a really dark cave. Porn slowly becomes like a drug for many people. You need porn to get aroused, then, you watch different kinds of porn because soft porn is no longer exciting. Porn often becomes an addiction and more and more men are becoming addicted to porn, and it's destroying their relationships.

Unfortunately, porn is so easily accessible and free!!!! When porn is no longer enough to watch, what happens next? Let me tell you what can happen and what has happened in my own relationship. My wonderful Christian Grey one night started talking about some of the porn scenes and how exciting it would be if we perhaps recreated the scenes in our own bed. He was referring then to having threesomes with another woman.

The Game Changer

Can you imagine how I felt then? I said to myself, "Oh my God, am I not enough for him? Am I not beautiful and sexy to him now? Don't I excite him anymore?" I now felt like I was not enough for him because if I were, he wouldn't want other women in our bed, would he? Of course, he always had the right words to say to make me feel better.

Cleverly, he said that if I were to do this it would be an experience of a lifetime for him and for us, and it would bring us even closer. I believed the crap he was feeding me. I went along with it after giving him certain rules that he could not break or else I would be out. He agreed to my rules at first. The challenge now was to try to find a willing participant that could be trusted because after all he was a fancy, well-respected businessman and he did not want any trouble like blackmail or scandal. He started looking for women on Craigslist, but they were not attractive, so he started looking at women who sell sex.

That's right. I know it's shocking but do you realize that there are so many other couples who are doing this and no one knows about it. So, we found a high-class escort that was more than willing to participate in the realization of a sexual fantasy. I remember the very first time, I felt nauseous and became sick before she arrived and had feelings of jealousy and the pain in my gut returned. I even heard a voice that said, "No, Lise this is wrong! Don't do this Lise!"

Pleasing my man was more important than anything else, and I went through with it. Afterward, I felt numb and disgusted. He paid a woman to have sex with us in our bed. This is not the Lise I used to know. Why did I do this? I felt so bad. It was all worth it in the end when the man of my dreams kept kissing me and saying that this was the best moment of his life and I was the only woman who was woman enough to do this with him. He told me that he loved me even more now and that he feels so much closer to me. That was all worth it then, right? I went above and beyond for my man, and now I am the best woman he'd ever had?

Lise Lavigne: 50 Shades of Wrong

My actions were out of love and a need to please the man I loved and desired. I was successful at making that happen. I didn't care about my own feelings in doing it. I overstepped on my values to please another and disregarded my intuition and ignored my inner guidance to accomplish this. I pleased another by having no respect for myself.

How many of us do this in our lives? We want so much to please others because we are seeking their love and approval and in so doing we neglect our own values, and we do it even though we don't agree with it. I learned this pattern very well as a child because I was sexually abused from the ages of three to twelve by various members of my family. This was just something I had been accustomed to in my life which is trying to please people for them to love me. With my Christian Grey, I just continued the pattern.

Remember earlier I mentioned that what happens is that people get used to something and want a bigger thrill, something more to excite them. Eventually, he wanted to experience bondage so whips and some physical pain occurred. It was all done in the name of sexual pleasure. Of course, there were more hiring of high-end escorts, and eventually one wasn't enough, he hired two of them, so there were more women.

It was getting further and further down the dark hole. He came up with even more fantasies he wanted to recreate in real life with me, and I was entertaining the idea of going further with him because I did not want to lose his love.

People say that porn is harmless; even relationship experts are advocating porn is healthy. I am telling you the opposite. That is nothing but a lie! Porn is the door to a very dark side that you have no idea where it could lead to. I am reminded of a story I heard about a frog in hot water. First, the frog is put in lukewarm water then the water gets warmer slowly. The frog has no clue this is happening and doesn't notice it. The water gets even warmer and warmer. The frog gets used to the temperature as it warms up and then the water reaches boiling point and the frog dies.

The Game Changer

All I wanted was to please my man, because I did not want to lose him. I wanted to make sure our sex life was the best because I didn't want him to cheat on me or leave me. I thought by allowing him to fulfill sexual fantasies that our relationship would flourish and we would be even more connected.

What a load of crap that was! I seriously believed this because my past created a woman of no value. My mindset was that of a woman who viewed herself as unworthy. I had no idea what a healthy relationship looked like; I had never experienced one. I had no example of one. I found my value in sex because that's what I was taught as a young child, to make my family members happy in my life I had to please them sexually. Their happiness was more important than my own if I wanted to be loved by them. So in my relationships, I again continued that pattern.

We are bombarded every day with images of how to look like and how to behave and sadly, young girls learn at a very young age to idolize the likes of certain celebrities who became famous for nothing other than having a private sex video released. Music videos are based on sexuality and not the actual music and lyrics. Everything in this world is sex, sex, sex. We are in the 21st century, and women are more sexualized than ever. Our young daughters are having sex as early as age six by giving blow-jobs to boys. This is the reality!!!

Let's not be as ostriches and not wake up to this very sad atrocity. Sex is everywhere. Everyone has sex, but few talk openly about it. Sex is like blowing your nose to some people, just another bodily function. But no, sex is something that brings two people together as one. Sex is beautiful and meaningful, and we need to start cherishing this moment.

We need to realize our worth and not give ourselves away to anyone just because and think it won't affect us. Women are not sexual objects. It took me a very long time to start believing that how I viewed myself affected the way I behaved and felt.

Lise Lavigne: 50 Shades of Wrong

The turning point in my life was when I found out that my so-called dream man ended up cheating on me anyways with other women including paying for sex on his own to fulfilled other fantasies that he knew I would definitely not allow.

Didn't I do all the things I did to keep him? Didn't he say I was the best girlfriend he'd ever had? You see, it doesn't matter to anyone what sacrifices you make. If you have very low esteem of yourself, you attract people who don't value you. All my life I thought everyone else was more important than I was and I would give and give and give until it hurt. That's what I did in this relationship yet again. I lost all sense of who I was, my own integrity compromised by myself. I violated my values. I did all of that to satisfy a man I was in love it.

When I discovered that he was on his own path of sexual perversion he wanted to explore on his own, I was crushed. My heart had never been so broken in my whole life. I cried a million tears. The pain I was suffering was unbearable. I was so close to grabbing a knife and stabbing it right into my heart to stop the pain.

But instead, I fell on my knees and cried out to God. I remember clearly, like it was yesterday. I said, "God help me! I don't want this life anymore. I want to do it your way from now on." It was at that moment that a feeling of peace and calm like I had never experience came over me. It was like the arms of God were comforting me. I fell asleep that night knowing that my life will never be the same again but I had no idea how.

Within days I came across a television program where a woman was talking about being sexually abused by her father. She was explaining the effects of these circumstances on her life. I immediately identified with what she was saying and had never heard anyone talk about this subject before. I realized by listening to her message that what had happened to me as a child caused me to have no self-worth whatsoever. The abuse that occurred in my life was certainly not something I focused on or thought about regularly; I never dwelt on it.

The Game Changer

In fact, it wasn't until I watched that television program that I started to think about it. I started to attend a church soon after and I attended a course that they were giving on how to overcome issues that you haven't been able to resolve. I decided to take that course to figure out why I was attracting one wrong relationship after the next.

I discovered that indeed I had lost all self-worth because of the abuse that happened at a very young age. I had learned to let people trample all over me. I felt damaged, tainted and broken all my life. I was holding onto a lot of shame because of it as well. I considered myself a piece of crap.

It wasn't until I learned that what happened was not my fault that I started to let go of the shame. I learned that my abusers didn't know any better themselves, so they were just perpetuating a cycle that others before them started. I, therefore, found compassion towards them and forgave them all. I then learned that even though I didn't get the love I needed as a child by my family, it didn't stop me from loving the wonderful person that I am. I realized that I am valuable and lovable. It was up to me to raise my standards according to my value.

The higher my value, the higher my standards became. I no longer accept anyone mistreating me because I now know that I am worth a lot more than that. I am a child of God after all. We really do teach others how to treat us. If someone is not treating us right, we don't have to accept it. We need to be clear on what our boundaries are to do that though. We also need to know how important and valuable we are as individuals and as women.

We don't need to dress provocatively to be attractive to the opposite sex. We can still look beautiful and sexy without showing so much skin for example. Believe me, I am not a prude, but if we dress a certain way we will attract a particular kind of person. If we dress without respecting ourselves, we will attract just that-people who don't respect us. Our beauty comes from the inside, it might be a cliché but it is the truth.

Whatever it is we feel inside is reflected to others whether you realize it or not. You think you can mask pain, guilt, anger, hatred, shame, sadness, low self-esteem but it is impossible to hide it. It all comes out one way or another. The energy that all of this has is sensed by other people's energy. Whatever energy you put out you will attract. It's as simple as that.

It took me such a long time to figure this out. As soon as I acquired this knowledge, I put it in practice as soon as possible. Let me tell you that it works. Once you deal with your past, and clean out the pain and hurt, your energy changes and circumstances improve pretty quickly.

For so long I was holding onto guilt and shame. I literally buried my head in the sand by ignoring the root cause of my troubles. I blamed everyone around me such as my family, my friends, my employers, my husband, and boyfriends.

I had to actually hit bottom with my pain so to speak before I decided to want to change my circumstances. Once I was willing to look at myself and the reason why all this was happening, that is when I accepted the fact that I might be the cause of it all. If I was the cause, it meant that I was responsible for it. If I was responsible for it, then I had the power to change it. I am so happy that I decided to accept what was going on and believed that only I had the power to make a difference in my own life- nobody else.

Yes, I have been sexually abused, and as a result, I suffered a lot in my life. I chose many wrong decisions because I did not know any better. I cannot go back in time and undo what I've done. I can't waste time regretting the bad choices I made either. What I can do though is break the cycle of the pain so that I can love others truly and the first person to start loving is myself. It took me over 40 years living in shame, guilt, and brokenness. I was keeping a lot of dirty secrets and the secrets accumulated to the breaking point. Once I released these secrets, my whole life transformed. Secrets kill!!! It will kill your relationships, your dreams, your peace, your joy and most importantly, it will kill who you truly are.

The Game Changer

Statistics show that one out of four women before the age of 18 has been sexually abused. It could be more than that as a lot of them do not report it. I know I didn't. If this has happened to you are not alone. Sexual assaults including rape are on the rise. This is affecting individuals which, in turns has an affect on families.

If families are affected, then societies are affected and so on. We might not be able to stop this sexual abuse cycle for good, but we can certainly stop the cycle in our own life. There is hope for people who have been through this. I know because I am living proof that life can be wonderful and totally different than what it used to be. We just need to want to make a change then make the right choice.

ABOUT THE AUTHOR

LISE LAVIGNE disrupts the status quo so that others can break free and flood the world with love. She does this by being a self-esteem coach, bestselling author, and motivational speaker. She works with women who want to gain more confidence and attract healthy relationships. Her passion is seeing the powerful transformation women make in their lives once they let go of their abusive past. She inspires and teaches women how to find peace and self-love.

Lise realized that women could take their power back and now she empowers others to do this as well. She is also the author of "Enough is Enough!" and the bestselling book "WOW Woman of Worth-Looking for Love in All the Wrong Places." She has created and launched an online program called Healthy Relationships Mastery. With her skills, love and compassion, Lise helps women restore their peace of mind and live victoriously.

Website: **www.liselavigne.com**
Instagram: @liselavigne_coaching
Facebook page: Lise Lavigne Coaching
Facebook Group: Healthy Relationships Mastery
https://www.facebook.com/groups/1860633337483692/

The Game Changer

MARILYN SUTHERLAND

My Journey to Lasting Love

I didn't know it, but I spent my entire life learning how to have love and partnership in my own life. In the process, I also learned how to coach other women in how to discover and nurture their own love journey.

SINGLE AND INDEPENDENT
My parents were married for over 50 years. My mom was generous, creative, kind and laughed easily. She was a great mom, and I wanted to be just like her except for one thing…I didn't want to get married. It seemed like my mom never got from dad what she really needed–to hear him say "I love you," and to feel adored. Dad was a man of integrity, hard-working and he didn't complain. He was the strong, silent type and could spend the whole evening and never talk.

After graduate school, I moved to Washington, D.C. for work. I would talk to my mom once or twice a week on the phone. I am Jewish, and my mom would always ask me if I was dating someone Jewish. My answer was usually "No." I dated nice guys who were not Jewish–partly so my mom wouldn't push me to get married. It seemed that marriage was a trap where women were expected to be a wife and mother, a cook and maid, and have a career. Several of my friends who were married didn't seem that happy, and a few were already divorced.

The Game Changer

In my early 30's, I was hired by IBM. My life was filled with exciting work and travel adventures including a 3-year assignment in California and a 15-month assignment in England where I visited a new city in Europe every six weeks.

I never thought of myself as someone looking for love since I did not want to settle down and get married. I jokingly described myself as an "independent woman who didn't need a man." Yet, I did yearn for a deep connection with a man who would be my partner in life. A committed, monogamous relationship remained elusive. All my relationships maxed out at two years.

I've participated in personal and organizational courses for over 30 years. From age 30 to 45, I worked on perfecting my "partner picker," and my picker did improve over time. With every relationship, I would learn something else about myself and how I saw love and commitment.

Nevertheless, I still had not found someone I could see being with, in a long-term relationship.

DO YOU LOVE ME?
Imagine you are standing with me in the front of a personal transformation course exploring how to live a life of growth and development. I know most of the people in the course. I'm standing in front of the group and sharing with everyone when one of the participants suddenly interrupts me. "Marilyn, ask us if we love you!"

"No, I'm not going to say that. I know everyone here doesn't love me." There is no way I would ask that question when I know the answer is, "No." Then one of my friends, who is sitting in the front row, looks up at me and whispers, "It's okay. Ask us."

I take a deep breath. I feel my cheeks getting hot and my heart pounding in my chest. I ask, "Do you love me?" After a few seconds of silence, everyone in the entire room stands up as one. Wow!

You'll never guess what I did in response to them standing to declare their love for me!

I call out to Mary who is visiting from another city, and ask why she is standing since she doesn't know me. She sweetly replies that I greeted her just before the course started and made her feel welcome. She assures me she would love me even more if she knew me better.

Hmm, okay. Who else could I challenge? I ask Phil, also visiting from another city, why he is standing since he doesn't know me.

Phil comes over to me, takes my hands in his and looks me in the eyes. It is such an intimate gesture, and totally unexpected. I start tearing up. "Marilyn, I'm getting married next month and what you shared about your life so far has helped me better understand my fiancé and our relationship. You have already contributed to me, and I've known you less than 24 hours!" I didn't know what to say. We hugged, and I whispered, "Thank you."

As Phil walks back to his seat, the course leader announces that we are taking a short break.

What happens next amazes me. Almost everyone in the room stands up and get in line-like a reception line-to personally hold my hands, look into my eyes and tell me why they stood.

I think they realized that this was an important learning for me and that if I was going to accept their expression of love, I needed to hear their specific reasons for standing. They waited patiently in line to tell me why they loved me. It was overwhelming. (Just writing this now, I'm getting teary-eyed, touched by their generosity over 20 years ago.)

A SERIES OF EPIPHANIES
That day was a life-changer for me. I could not believe that I had challenged

The Game Changer

Mary and Phil for standing up to show their love for me. I had basically called them liars, and they were both so gracious with me.

My big insight? I was actively rejecting love that didn't match my expectations. I said I wanted a life filled with love yet, when love showed up; I had pushed it away. Where else had I pushed love away because it didn't match my expectations?

A few weeks later, I drove to my parents' house from Washington, D.C., for the weekend. Mom and I are running errands, and she tells me she has been feeling lonely because Dad watches TV, and reads all day and doesn't interact with her. I had heard this for years and finally said, "Mom, do you want to come and live with me?" "No, I don't want to leave your dad. I love him. I just want you to listen. All my friends are widows, and if I say anything about your dad, they just tell me I'm lucky he's alive. Just listen, honey." All these years I thought my mom was not happy. Now I realized she just needed to vent. Hmmm, maybe marriage is not a trap...

This discovery opened me up to an even more important revelation. Looking back over the last ten years, I realized that I never allowed myself to be vulnerable, to open my heart to love and to risk being hurt. Maybe my story about being an independent woman who didn't need a man was a way of protecting myself from the disappointment in love that I mistakenly thought was my mom's situation.

From that moment on, I started letting love in wherever it showed up. When I was walking down the hall at work, I would look at the person approaching me, smile and say "hello." I experienced our connection– human being to human being. When I would hug my friends and family, I would experience the love as I was saying and hearing the words. (Now I know I was reprogramming my brain to receive and express love.)

I started being open to others in a way I had never done before. It felt like I was filling up the empty holes in my heart with love, from playing hide-and-seek with a baby at the table next to me to feeling an instant connection with a woman colleague I met at a networking event. Every connection was a form of love no matter who it was from. I welcomed it all into my heart. I started expressing my love for others without the expectation that my love would be reciprocated.

STOP WAITING FOR THE ONE and START LIVING
One final realization occurred a few weeks after I started letting love in my life. I asked myself, "If I wasn't waiting for 'the one,' what would I be doing?" My answer was to get a Ph.D. in organizational development. I'd never allowed myself to think about going back to school because, whenever I would start dating a new guy, I was always so busy with work, volunteering, travel, and friends that he would complain. I thought being in graduate school would make it even harder for me to find love. I had put my love of learning on hold, just in case I met someone.

That Monday, I called a professor from a Ph.D. program at George Washington University and found out that I had missed the deadline for applying - not just for George Washington but for most graduate programs nationally. Most schools were now accepting applications for the following September. The professor recommended a new program at George Mason University (GMU) just starting up, that might still be accepting applications.

I called and reached the GMU director, and after talking for about 20 minutes, he invited me to join the program. He knew my boss at IBM and the project I was working on and was clear I would be a valuable addition to the class. All I had to do was come the next day to fill out the paperwork. When I told him my intention to get a Ph.D., he explained this was a Master's program. I already had a Master's degree in another field, so I didn't need another one. He explained that completing a year of his program would make me more competitive if I applied to a Ph.D. program the following year. Convinced it was a smart move, I showed up the next day to complete the paperwork, and three days later I was attending my first class.

I loved being in school and was excited about my next career. If I didn't have a partner who loved me, it was okay—I was learning to let love in my life from friends and family.

LOVE FINDS ME and I'M READY
In 1987, I started volunteering at a non-profit organization called RESULTS. That first year I met Chuck Sutherland at the annual conference in Washington, D.C., when we would lobby Congress on hunger and poverty issues. Chuck and I had spoken to each other every year at the conference and had a friendly exchange. Ten years later, we were chatting at the conference. I asked him if I could record our conversation for a paper I was writing about RESULTS for one of my graduate school courses. I recorded our conversation and sent Chuck a transcript several weeks later.

Chuck called me several days later. We discussed the transcript; then he mentioned that he was getting a divorce. I told him I was sorry, and he said it was a good thing since his second wife had never bonded with his children. Then I said, "Well, that means you're available." Chuck immediately replied, "Is that an offer?"

I was trying to be supportive that he could now find a great woman to be his partner in parenting his children. I wasn't interested in him. Over the years I had dated several men who were separated and now had a rule to wait a year after their divorce. Chuck had only been separated about a month. Other factors were that Chuck had five children and three lived in Dallas, he lived in Wichita, Kansas, and was working in St. Louis while I lived in Washington, DC.

I didn't know what to say to Chuck and wasn't even sure he was serious, so I replied ,"Okay." I went on to share with him my journey that I just shared with you about how I was finally a happy single and how I wished that for him. I was totally myself, no pretense. We spoke for over two hours about our lives and our work.

The next evening Chuck called me back and told me how much he enjoyed our conversation–and I agreed. It was the most fun phone call I had had with a man in years. Then he asked me if I was interested in going out. I stopped before I responded. Chuck was a nice guy, and we had a lot in common–we were both committed to RESULTS, microcredit, child health, and primary education in the U.S., and worldwide. We had both participated in personal development programs. He was a lifelong learner like me. He was a talker (not like my dad). I liked him, and what was the harm? After all, I wasn't going to marry him! I answered, "Yes."

We talked every night for 2-3 hours for a month before our first date in St. Louis. We saw each other every 2-3 weekends. After our first date, I went home for the weekend and was talking to Chuck. My mom overheard me and asked me if he was a comedian. I reminded her he's a real estate developer. She told me she never heard me laugh so much with a guy.

Our third date was Thanksgiving at my house in D.C. Chuck flew in from Wichita, and my parents drove in from Pittsburgh. After we all settled in, my mom asked Chuck, "What makes you such a great catch. You've been divorced twice." Oh, no! I cannot believe my mom said that. Chuck's response was priceless. He said, "Your daughter is an amazing woman, and I'm so happy that, after all these years we have connected. She makes me a better man." Mom never said another word about his divorces.

After dating six months, we decided to get married. Remember how my mom wanted me to date someone Jewish? Mom never said a word about the fact that he was raised Catholic. She did ask that we have a Jewish officiant perform the service and we did.

The fears I had about being married fell away. I hit the jackpot–he was smart, interesting, well-read, loving and forgiving, creative, funny, kind, successful, accepting, and supportive of whatever I did (and he still is). I had finally perfected my "partner picker." What I valued in Chuck reflected the same values I had for friends.

What's surprising is that the things that made him a non-potential for dating on our first call (nice but no attraction, five children, lived in another city and was recently separated) were non-issues after we had our initial conversations. I had made a core connection with him that made those concerns irrelevant.

When I completed my Master's program, nine months after our first phone conversation, I sold my house and moved from Washington to Dallas, Texas, where three of his children lived. I wanted to support him in having a relationship with his kids and knew if I stayed in Washington, he wouldn't see his kids much since we would want to be together on weekends.

MARRIED WITH CHILDREN

Almost a year after our phone call, we got married. I became an instant step-mother to five children aged 16-25, and a grandmother to a 9-month-old granddaughter.

New husband, new job, new family, new friends, new city, new everything. Wow! Then a week after my wedding, my mother died unexpectedly. I was very close to my mom, and this was devastating. That first year of marriage was both the happiest and the saddest year of my life.

Until Chuck, I never fully committed to a relationship and never dated a man longer than two years. I always had my own place where I could get away, but now I had no backup plan.

Despite years of being an expert in business relationships and communication, I had no clue how to create a loving relationship day-to-day…but, thankfully, Chuck did. (When he read this, he burst out laughing and said, "I think you should rewrite this to say that after two divorces, I had learned a lot about what not to do in a marriage).''

I had to learn relationship habits for lasting love. All my dating had prepared me for was dating. My dating life had not prepared me for being in a loving relationship with a commitment to making a relationship work.

Marilyn Sutherland: My Journey to Lasting Love

FROM 'ME' TO 'WE' and INSTANT FAMILY
During the first few years I was married, my life felt unreal. I was an east coast girl living in Texas. That "independent woman" was now married, had children from 16 to 25, and was a grandma. It didn't feel like my life anymore. I wasn't prepared for the changes in every aspect of my life.

It wasn't easy for me–learning how to be one-half of a couple. Learning to be a stepmom. Learning to live with someone 24/7 after living alone for most of my adult life. Learning to manage money as a couple (I was risk-adverse, and he had a high tolerance for risk as a real estate investor/developer). And the list goes on. More importantly, I learned to give up being an "independent woman," and become a true partner with Chuck.

In truth, it took years for me to become the kind of partner who put our love and our relationship first. It was a process for me to evolve from "me," to "you and me," then finally to "we."

As someone who was single for over two decades and is now married for almost two decades, I first had to learn how to be a happy single, loving my life and then how to be a happy wife, step-mother, and grandmother (we now have eight grandchildren from 8 to 19 years old). Thankfully, my mom was a great role model for mothering.

WHAT WE PRACTICE GROWS STRONGER
I believe that what we practice grows strong. If we want loving relationships, then we must practice being loving every day. We can't wait until our soulmate shows up to start being loving or happy or, (fill in the blank with what your heart desires).

I'm committed to practicing living from love every day, to be the best partner to Chuck, my family, friends, colleagues, and my clients.

My friends were right when they told me, "When you give up looking for love, love will find you." When I started practicing being loving, I opened myself to the love that was already in my life. I started living my best life and two years after that life-changing day; I attracted my future husband.

Men who are healthy want healthy, happy, confident women who are ready and willing to give and receive love. I love to help single women discover how to be healthy, happy and confident. When they do, they attract the love they want from healthy men. I love to support women who are in committed relationships or married to elevate their relationships and bring back that loving feeling so they are creating, attracting and experiencing the love they want with their partner every day.

My journey of lasting love started with loving "me," and has evolved to "we."

How will your journey evolve?

Marilyn Sutherland

About the Author

MARILYN SUTHERLAND is the founder of Free to Create coaching, training people in the essential skills to have powerful, sustaining relationships in every area of life.

She is the creator of the relationship program "Your Journey to Lasting Love." Women gain mastery in being a whole human being (mind, body, heart, and spirit) to become happier and more confident and attract and sustain the relationships they desire and deserve.

In 2018, Marilyn will publish a book on love relationships based on almost 100 in-depth interviews with men and women from ages 20 to 75+. This book will help you navigate your journey of love by learning from others' successes and challenges.

In business, she coaches managers to successfully lead change initiatives built on trust, and communication. She helps employees discover how to show up as leaders and build solid professional relationships within and outside of their organization.

Marilyn had a 17-year career at IBM including as a manager and relationship manager. After obtaining a Master's degree in Organizational Development, she worked for Accenture as a Change Management Specialist.

She had her own business for years, consulting in change, organizational design, management and human resources. As a leader of personal transformational seminars for 12 years, she coached over 1,000 individuals to be in powerful action to fulfill their dreams.

The Game Changer

She is a graduate of Presence-Based Leadership Coach Training. Marilyn is now a relationship expert at **www.YourTango.com**.

If you would like to know more about how Marilyn could empower you in your relationship, please contact her at **Marilyn@FreeToCreate.net**.

PAT IYER
From Near Bankruptcy to Millions

I felt my body tremble as I was ushered into the office of the Dean of the School of Nursing of the University of Pennsylvania I attended. It seemed like the office was the size of a football field. I eased into the chair opposite the dean's desk and took a deep breath.

"What can I do for you, Pat?"

"I came to ask for money. I'm broke."

I was a 28-year-old graduate student who had an incredible professional opportunity and no resources to be able to take advantage of it.

My husband was fired from a well-paying job the week after I entered graduate school the year before. The firing took us completely off guard. I had quit my job to go to graduate school full time. My education was funded by government scholarships. We had just been about to put our entire savings into buying land for investment purposes. Suddenly he had no job; I was in school full time, and we had no income. We had a 2-year-old son.

During the year I was in school, my husband put together funding to buy a welding business in an urban New Jersey City. For that entire year, we

The Game Changer

lived off the money we would have spent on the land. Week after week I watched our checking account steadily dwindle.

Part of my graduate program involved developing a plan to teach pregnant diabetics. My professor encouraged me to write an abstract for an upcoming meeting of the American Diabetes Association. I realized I did not fully understand what I was volunteering to do when my abstract was accepted, and I received an invitation to make a presentation to the attendees of the American Diabetes Association conference in Beverly Hills, California. The conference was taking place a few weeks after I graduated in May 1979.

We had $200 left when I graduated. How could I accept the offer? I had no money for a plane ticket, no money for a hotel, no credit card, and no cash for food. The timing was terrible, yet it was such an honor to be invited, that I wanted to accept. I asked my professor, "What do I do? How can I fund this?" "Ask the dean of the school of nursing for money," she advised me. "She loves to promote the school and improve its image. She would give you money."

The dean was an aloof, imposing figure I had seen only from a distance. I was aware of her reputation as being forward thinking. Frankly, she intimidated me–how could I consider asking her for money? The week after I graduated with my master's degree in nursing, I started a job as a director of staff development in a large urban hospital. I asked my boss if the hospital would fund my trip to California to make this presentation. "We'll let you have time off to go even though you have not worked here long enough to be eligible for vacation time, but we won't pay your expenses."

With no other choice, I made an appointment with the dean. She listened to my request. There was a small smile on her face. "I think your employer should pay your expenses," she told me. "I tried that and found out they'd give me the time off but not pay for my airfare of hotel. Here's what I can do. I will call guidance counselors and alumni of the University of

Pennsylvania who live in the Beverly Hills area. I will explain why I am at the conference and praise the educational opportunities at the school."

The dean's eyes started sparkling. "Yes, I think we can support that." She arranged for me to get a print out of alumni and said that when I prepared a report of my activities in California, she would issue a check for $400.

As I walked out of her office, I shook my head in wonder. "I just asked the dean of the University of Pennsylvania School of Nursing for money, and she agreed!" It was one of the biggest risks I had taken in my life. For me to walk into that office, I had to admit I needed help. That was not an easy step for me. My mother's Irish English heritage dominated the values in our family. The British stiff upper lip philosophy did not encourage admitting to making mistakes or needing help. "Just deal with it. You'll survive," was a more common message than, "How can I help?"

I experienced a glow of satisfaction when the check for $400 arrived after I submitted my report of the phone calls I made in California. I took a risk; it paid off. I began receiving paychecks from the hospital, and my husband took a temporary job while he focused on raising money to buy a welding company.

Borrowing a Million Dollars
Just about a year later, in May 1980, my husband completed arranging for loans from a venture capital company and the Minority Small Business Administration. He needed a million dollars to start his company. And we did not have it. For an entire day, we signed papers to borrow the money. The lenders explained the meaning of each paper. "This one is a personal guarantee. It means that if you default on the loan payments, everything you own can be taken." My husband and I exchanged glances, picked up the pens and signed.

"This is a description of the loan payments and interest rate. You'll be paying 24 percent interest rate each month." What we did not realize as we signed that document was that there was no way the company could be successful enough to repay the loan. We just doomed ourselves and the company to failure.

The company started on an optimistic note. The mayor of the city came to a ribbon cutting, and my husband talked about the jobs his business would create. We feasted on catered food, and then the realities of running a welding business took over: hiring people, buying equipment, getting customers and dealing with problems. We got phone calls in the middle of the night: "This is your security company. Your building has been broken into."

My husband would get up and drive to his building to look at the damage. In one incident, a camera my father gave my husband was stolen. The thieves pulled all of the papers out of his filing cabinet and threw them all over the floor. In another break-in, the thieves stole the personal tools of the workers.

Our young son rarely saw his father. My husband worked seven days a week. I found weekend activities to keep my son busy. We thought, "We'll have our second child after the business is stable, doing well, and making money." My husband worked harder, longer hours, but the problems continued. His second in command was not a good manager, was forgetful, and couldn't control the operations. There was a snake in the building, a mouse in the copier, an employee with addiction issues, a near-fatal accident with a gas cylinder, and an incident with pipes that rolled off a truck while it was in traffic.

And another call in the middle of the night, "Mr. Iyer, your building is on fire." A day before Thanksgiving, the thieves set the wooden back door of the building on fire, thinking they would burn their way into the building. A train conductor saw the fire and called the fire department. My husband called 20 companies to find one who would board up the door.

Pat Iyer: From Near Bankruptcy to Millions

In the midst of the struggles at my husband's business, my son's friend's father said to me, "Oh, your husband owns his own business. That means he is his own boss. He sets his hours." The stars in his eyes triggered an emotional response from me, "Oh, yes. He is his own boss. He gets to work seven days a week, and there is no one there to tell him it is time to go home. His son rarely sees him. We have not had a vacation in 4 years. We have a huge debt to repay. You've got four small children. Think twice about starting a company." He backed away from me, sorry he had said anything.

By 1982, it was obvious to my husband and me that he could not keep the company afloat. The interest alone was killing his dream. I was pregnant with our second son when my husband began negotiating with the lenders to see how we could escape from the crushing debt. The lenders, reminding him of the personal guarantee we had signed, sent an appraiser to our house to determine its market value. My husband followed him around pointing out all of the flaws of the house, to diminish its value in the event they decided to take it from us. I envisioned living on the street with my newborn in a cardboard box.

As a result of effective negotiation skills, my husband was able to extricate us from the business debts we had, avoid declaring bankruptcy and close down the business. Within weeks he started a business as a manufacturer's representative and was able to run it out of our living room–without an office building, employees, or debt. He continued to run his business, and I continued to work in staff development until 1986 when I changed jobs.

A Seminar that Changed My Life
In the spring of 1987, I sat in a conference room listening to a nurse talk about career alternatives for nurses. I was employed as a nursing quality assurance coordinator and enjoyed the analysis of trends and development of plans to improve care. But I was traveling 1.25 hours one way a day on the most heavily trafficked roads in New Jersey and was getting burned out from the trip. The title of the seminar caught my attention. At that point,

The Game Changer

I had been out of nursing school for about 20 years and had been a staff nurse, diploma school educator, nursing staff development director, and nursing quality assurance coordinator.

The seminar leader presented information about a number of non-traditional nursing roles. She explained that nurses went to court to testify about standards of care. That sounded very interesting. I had a master's degree in nursing, had co-authored a book about the nursing process, had experience teaching staff nurses and department managers and liked to write. I had years of staff nurse experience in medical-surgical nursing and maintained clinical involvement while I directed the hospital's staff development department.

The next day when I returned to work, I called the attorney who ran the hospital's risk management department. I asked him how I could get into expert witness work. He explained about my state's jury verdict analysis publication and Martindale Hubbell (now martindale.com) as a way to connect with attorneys. My life changed forever when I walked into the country courthouse's library. I used the jury verdict analysis issues in the library to determine which attorneys were doing nursing or medical malpractice cases. I copied down information from a directory of attorneys. When I had a list of about 20 attorneys, I sent out an introduction letter that explained that I was available to review medical, surgical cases as a nursing expert witness, enclosed my CV and sat back to see what would happen.

In the meantime, I decided to quit my job. I planned to start a business by piecing together sources of income: consulting with hospitals on quality assurance and documentation issues, being a part-time staff nurse, writing books, and teaching seminars for a national seminar company. I took a leap of faith that was amazing considering that we faced near bankruptcy five years earlier when my husband's business failed. That experience made me determined not to borrow any money to start a business. (To this day, I have never borrowed money to keep my business going.) I set up my desk in the corner of our family room: my first desk was a board placed over the tops of two 2-drawer filing cabinets.

Expert witness work begins.
What I did not realize when I sent out those letters was that medical-surgical units were (and are) frequently the targets of suits. Attorneys needed nursing experts and lots of them. People with my background were not common, and immediately I got the attention of two defense attorneys; one in October 1987 and one in November 1987. The first one sent a case that was easy to defend. It involved a young girl who fainted in the bathroom and cut her knee on the smashed glass IV bottle. I wrote a report which included citations to medical literature. I'd never seen an expert witness report and did not understand what he needed. Then I got a phone call from the defense attorney. "Pat, I like your report, but the format is wrong. We have to work on that." I revised the report and sent it off.

Within a few months, my client called me. He was laughing, and said the case was "dismissed with prejudice." He explained that after the plaintiff attorney got my report, he took out his checkbook and wrote his client a check and asked her to forget her suit. I found out this was very uncommon (and have not heard of it happening since then!)

The second attorney, who contacted me in November 1987, told me he was defending a licensed practical nurse (LPN) who worked the night shift. A confused elderly man had walked out of the hospital one cold March evening on the evening shift, in his patient gown, and was knocking on doors in the neighborhood. The police brought him back, and the doctor wrote an order for chest and wrist restraints. The LPN went into the room with the RN who was assigned to him and made sure he was in his chest restraint. The LPN went to tend her wing of patients. This patient got out of bed within 30 minutes, untied his chest restraint, removed the window screen, walked out onto the hospital roof, and fell into the parking lot in front of the emergency department. He survived his fall and died later from his cancer. The attorney casually mentioned in his November 1987 phone call that trial was set for two months later.

First trial
After I wrote my report defending the LPN, the attorney called me up to discuss scheduling for trial. I remember being floored and calling a friend in a panic. "I wanted to be an expert witness, but I never thought I'd have to testify in the second case I reviewed!" I think I could have gotten to the courthouse on sheer adrenaline on the day of trial, without needing my car. The defense attorney led me through the direct exam, and then the plaintiff attorney stood up to cross-examine me. I looked at him with dread. He asked only one question: "Was there any documentation the wrist restraints were placed on the patient?" "No," I told him. When the defense attorney called after the trial was over, I put him on speaker phone and my husband and son rejoiced to hear that the jury let the LPN off (the RN was held liable, but the award was small.)

That initial batch of twenty letters continued to bring me work, repeat business, word of mouth referrals and my expert witness caseload grew.

Expert witness referral business starts Med League Support Services
One day in 1989, I got a critical phone call. A plaintiff attorney asked me to review an emergency department nursing case. "I'm not an ED nurse," I told him, "but I know a Masters-prepared clinical specialist who would be great." I connected the two of them, sat back, and the light bulb went off. I had done both of them a favor without any financial compensation. "Could there be a business in referring expert witnesses?" I wondered. It turns out there was, and that revelation made me a millionaire.

Earlier in my life, I had been involved in two multi-level marketing companies. One sold cleaning products; the other sold cosmetics. These compa nies provided excellent training about sales and business structure. What I learned from those experiences was:

Pat Iyer: From Near Bankruptcy to Millions

1. Your income is limited by the number of hours you can work. If others are working for you, you can get a piece of other people's hours.

2. When you are marketing, you have to develop a hard shell. Each "no" brings you closer to the person who will say "yes." You learn to say, "Next."

3. I was not destined to sell soap or cosmetics. I knew I could do more with my healthcare background.

After this request for an ED nurse, I formed Med League Support Services as a sole proprietorship. Using the relationships I had built up over the years, I began to recruit nurses to review cases for me. The first expert I got under contract was the ED nurse.

In the beginning, I assumed that all of my experts could write well. A few years later, I got another life-changing phone call. One of my clients complained about the semi-literate report he'd received from one of my experts. I was horrified when I saw what she had put together. After that, I insisted the experts send the reports to me for proofreading. I picked up issues that needed to be resolved before the report could be presented to the attorney and developed resources for training the experts. This quality control measure strengthened my experts' reports and helped build my company's reputation for providing quality experts.

Initially, my business was located in my house. We lived at 55 Britton Road, so I added Suite 500 to the address. At first, my husband and I tried to share a computer. That was short-lived. Then we turned the family room into my husband's office and put a desk in the living room. We had two kids under the age of 9. The workday never ended; I worked all day and into the evening. One day my youngest son, who was three, asked me for something and without turning around, I told him (rather self-righteously, I'm afraid) that I could not help him. "I am working." He burst into tears and told me, "I feel like such a pest." That was the moment I realized I had to hire a part-time employee so I could free up some time.

The Game Changer

Moving out
One day my husband said, "Our youngest son does not need a bedroom. I could use his bedroom for an office." I insisted our child needed a bed and a room of his own, so we bought a house 10 miles away and turned the first house into an office house. We had three employees coming in (two of mine, one of his) for two years until a neighbor reported us for violating the zoning rules. Fortunately, we had already made an offer to purchase a 3,600 square feet office condo. The zoning officer took pity on us and did not close our businesses down, and within a month, we had moved out of the office house into the office condo. My husband and I bought the condo and rented it to our businesses. It was a very wise financial move. The rent we took paid for the condo three times over.

Selling a Personal Service Business
After growing the company to the point of consistently billing more than a million dollars a year for five years in a row, I decided to look for a buyer. Although I tried on my own to locate a buyer, I was not successful until I hired a business broker. He worked with me to develop a package to present to potential buyers. What I learned to emphasize is that the company was not me. It did not rest on my skills. My company had 200 expert witnesses under contract to review cases, a robust private training site for our experts, a large database of repeat clients, and a steady stream of cases. It had solid cash flow and provided me as the owner with a significant amount of compensation. I built an appealing legacy business.

After a year of working with the business broker, being interviewed by a few dozen prospects and receiving several offers, I sold Med League on January 2, 2015. It was a tremendous feeling to know that the work I did owner, employees, subcontractors, and clients.

I now do what I love: ghostwriting, editing and mentoring others.

Pat Iyer: From Near Bankruptcy to Millions

Building a Successful Business
Here are conclusions I reached about building a strong business.

1. If at all possible, create your business launch so that you are not under pressure to make a profit right away. It takes more time than you would expect to market and start attracting clients. When I started Med League, my husband was bringing in enough money that I could take my time and be self-employed through teaching nurses, consulting with hospitals, and expert witness work. Gradually I centered on working with attorneys as my primary source of income.

2. Learn the nuances of marketing and writing appealing copy for brochures and websites. Your prospect is bombarded with information. You have to capture that person's attention quickly and in a compelling way. I have studied this aspect of running a business and invested thousands of dollars in courses, mentors, and books to learn more about marketing. The more you understand about marketing, the more comfortable and confident you feel.

3. Pick the right service that fits your strengths. Know what you are good at and recognize that it cannot be at all aspects of running a business. Find others to help you.

4. Never stop marketing and don't rely on only one client for work.

5. Pay attention to relationships. Your clients want to work with people they know, like and trust. Look for ways to build strong relationships with your clients so that they would not dream of working with another person.

6. Use honest and ethical business practices. You have to be able to look yourself in the mirror and be proud of your ethics.

7. Avoid borrowing money if you can. Use your revenues, not loans,

to invest in your business such as upgrading your computer equipment.

8. Charge reasonable fees that the market will bear. Do not join the rush to the bottom to undercut your competitors. You will destroy your business by performing work at the lowest rate on the market, find it impossible to raise fees, and run out of money.

9. Consider the multiple ways you can reach your market: a website, a blog, tweets, Facebook, e-zines, emails, videos, and video testimonials. Use these methods to remind your client base of your existence. Use principles of crafting effective marketing messages and consistently implement them.

10. "Hire slowly, fire quickly." There is a great deal of wisdom in that expression. Carefully screen employees. A typo on a resume is enough for me to set it aside. I have fired employees for absenteeism, incompetence, and poor attitude. Be grateful when a marginal employee quits. Although it causes short-term disruption, it is far better for a person to self-select out of your system. Don't tolerate marginal work performance. There are far better people looking for work.

11. Use financial controls in your business. Avoid providing embezzlement and theft opportunities. When you have employees, have one person open the mail, and another person deposits the money. Do not allow employees to sign checks; no one should be able to sign except for the owner. (One of my colleagues caught an employee buying a personal computer charged to the company credit card. The employee counted on the owner not looking at the credit card bill. It was a fluke that the owner saw the bill and caught the purchase.) Allow only extremely trustworthy employees to access bank accounts. Be very careful about allowing employees to remotely access your server. Someone could secure a laptop or desktop computer in an employee's home and gain access to the company's data. And if that

employee quits or gets fired, how will you keep your data safe?

12. Your employees are not your friends. Do not be overly generous. Be fair, be aware of the labor laws, and be careful with benefits and bonuses.

13. Starting a business is hard and not for everyone. Be prepared to sacrifice, to work long hours and to learn continuously. Entrepreneurship gets into your blood as you begin to experience the joys of being your own boss.

ABOUT THE AUTHOR

PATRICIA IYER, MSN RN LNCC is the former president of Med League Support Services, Inc., an independent legal nurse consulting firm she established in 1989. Pat ran this company for 28 years before selling it in January 2015. She is past president of the American Association of Legal Nurse Consultants.

A prolific author, Pat is the editor, author or coauthor of over 800 books, articles, online courses, case studies or chapters. She also works with people who have books inside them and with Pat's help, become published authors. Pat is a ghostwriter and mentor for people who do not have the time or skills to write a book.

See **www.PatIyer.com** for editing services information.

Also, Pat provides education and mentoring for legal nurse consultants who want to skyrocket their businesses through her programs at **www.legalnursebusiness.com** and **www.LNCAcademy.com**.

QUYNH VO
Never Good Enough

I dedicate this story to my husband who is the wind beneath my wings. You are truly my better half.

THE VERDICT

There I was, sitting in the Dean's waiting room. My mind was racing, and my heart was about to jump out of my chest. I had been dreading this moment, since I skipped writing my two final exams for my 1st year pharmacy program at U of A. All the finals were in April, but I was so sick from cramming for exams the last two weeks of school that I managed to get a doctor's note, and got permission to write them a few weeks later. The problem was, they happened to be on the same day of my Buddhist youth group's world jamboree camp. And I didn't know when the next camp like this would happen again…if ever.

I tried to move the make-up finals but I couldn't because it was only available that one time, and every student who missed it the first time would have to write it then.

I was stuck in a dilemma. But I had to make a decision: school or pleasure. My fate, my destiny was going to be determined in the next few minutes.

The Game Changer

It rested entirely in the hands of the Dean, and there was nothing I could do about it.

Have you ever felt so powerless in a situation and you wish you had more strength, more power, more control?

Well, I gave up that right when I decided fun was more important. After all, school will always be there, but this camp only happens this year, and it might never happen again.

Have you ever done something knowing full well that this short-term pleasure is going to bite you in the ass later? That it will come back with a vengeance and you will have to pay the price?

I made my choice-a decision that took me on a different path, a path that to this day I still wonder, who in their right mind would do such a thing? Well, I did! And I was a typical A student that any parents would be proud to have.

The door opened, and my heart stopped.

I felt like I was being called into the execution chamber.

I didn't want to be here. I wanted to run, but it was too late.

The next few minutes were a blur. Partly because my mind couldn't take it, and partly because I was tearing up. I didn't know what to say. I had no defense. I hadn't thought of this consequence.

I was kicked out of Pharmacy school because my mark was too low. It was a sentence that was more mortifying to me than death. At least, if I had died, I'd only have to suffer that one moment in time, and then that's it. But now, I have to live with this consequence, and I have to tell my mom.

I cried like a baby.

In a matter of minutes, I had aged years, maybe even decades. I was 19, and I felt I wanted to die.

All I can remember is REGRET and FEAR.

THE MASK

Have you ever done something that you would never tell another soul because you're afraid they'll judge you? Something you did? Or something that happened to you?

I was so ashamed. I was so lost and scared. But I kept the problem to myself. I tried to solve the problem by myself, and I was alone in this journey. I pretended everything was fine. I put on a happy face so that nobody would find out.

Had I been a bad student; had I been an average student; this would not have been a problem. I was one of those students that every kid hates. Well not really hate, but more like love to hate. My friends would have to study for weeks, and all I needed was a couple of days cramming, and I would be getting better marks than them. (By the way - I've learned not to be the smartest person in the room and surround myself with people smarter than me.)

That kind of work ethic didn't serve me too well in university. But I was so good at cramming that it worked. It was enough to get me accepted into the Pharmacy program after just one year of general science.

That wasn't the case anymore after I got into Pharmacy. I was competing with all these other smart kids. And my study habits brought me mostly B's and C's in this class. And missing the two finals brought me 2 F's, and that's why I was kicked out of Pharmacy.

My entire identity was wiped out.

All of a sudden I'm a NOBODY!

The Game Changer

Well no, it's much worse. I'm a FAILURE!

I couldn't tell anyone my secret.

I couldn't tell anyone the truth.

So I put on the mask.

THE SECOND LIFE

If cats have nine lives to live, I wonder how many lives we humans get? Because I think I died in the Dean's room and emerged a different person. My innocence was gone. My days of care-free and worry-free were gone. I became a person who cared more about what other people might think of me than what I think of myself.

Have you ever really wanted to impress someone so much and all you wanted was their approval and to hear that they're proud of you? Who is that person to you? Your dad? Your mom? Your husband? Your wife? Your children?

Well for me that person, is definitely, my mom.

I put my mom on a pedestal because she's a phenomenal human being. The sacrifice she made for her children, is a debt I could never repay. She was strict and controlling. Well, she had to be that way because it was for our survival. Our country was at war. People were starving. The south of Vietnam had lost the war. We escaped by boat, and we made it to Canada. That was a miracle in itself. Many people died at sea. We survived, and we had to start over empty-handed here in this new country we now call home.

My mom was a teacher in Vietnam. And she was as good as it gets outside and inside, at work and home. She always put her children first. I never felt poor or insecure throughout my childhood. She protected us so well that I had never felt the impact of the war or the hardships that we endured.

Quynh Vo: Never Good Enough

She gave up the life in Vietnam where she was revered and admired so that her children could have a better life in Canada, or anywhere else for that matter.

The first few years were hard for my parents.

I don't know how many lives she'd been through by the time we got to Canada, but my mom was lucky to find a job as a kitchen helper in a restaurant. Problem is she was too small, too slow, and too weak to do a lot of the work there. But she was such a hard worker that they couldn't let her go. She would work through lunch and dinner because she saw so much work still had to be done. Her boss and coworkers would often have to remind her to eat. Otherwise, she would just skip lunch or dinner to catch up with all the work.

My dad drove a taxi, and he worked around the clock, only coming home to shower and sleep. I rarely saw him at home. He'd be gone by the time I woke up to go to school, and I'd be sleeping by the time he got home.

They both worked hard to give us a good life, and my brothers and I know it.

Our only job was to do well in school.

It was hard for us, too.

I remember crying in the school's washroom, on the school bus, and at night because I felt so lost in school. I didn't understand what the teachers were saying. I left Vietnam when I was 11 years old, attending grade 6, and by the time I arrived in Canada, after two years staying at a refugee camp, I was tested and placed in grade 8. I was good at math, but everything else was a struggle. I didn't understand what my classmates were saying either. I felt like an outsider. I had no friends.

So I studied hard until English was no longer a problem. And school was no longer a challenge.

And I knew my responsibility – I had to be a good student so that I can have a good career and a good life.

LIES, LIES & LIES
I remember how proud my mom was when I got accepted into the Pharmacy program at U of A. Her dream was to be one, but in Vietnam, she didn't have the money to go to that school, so she had to settle to become a teacher instead. And here I am, fulfilling that dream for her. I was going become a pharmacist.

But now I'd been kicked out of the program.

If this gets out, I'd be her source of shame instead of pride.

How can I break her heart? How can I tell her what happened?

I couldn't bring myself to tell her the truth. I was afraid to tell her the truth.

I struggled on my own.

I went on going to school as usual, as if nothing had happened. My mom had no idea.

My friends knew I wasn't in Pharmacy anymore because I couldn't hide that fact. But I never told them that I was kicked out. I told them "I don't like it – it was too boring for me" (it was true, but it was based on a lie so I could hide the shame). I planned to finish my bachelor of science and try to get in Medicine or Dentistry instead. "I'm gonna aim higher"- that was my plan to redeem myself.

The problem is, I was lost. I was scared. I was ashamed. I was alone.

I put on the mask to protect myself. I built a wall between everyone else and me.

Nobody knew how much I was suffering because I hid it so well. I fooled others, but I couldn't fool myself.

Have you ever told a lie, and that one lie lead to another lie, and another lie, and before you know it you forgot what the truth actually is?

Now, this could be as simple as you telling a lie to cover your ass as I did. Or it can be as complicated and convoluted as telling yourself a lie because you don't want to face the truth or do anything about it.

I acted like I had it all together when I didn't. I acted like I was happy when I wasn't.

I just got really good at telling lies to myself. I don't know when it started, but I began to dislike myself.

It's hard enough to be yourself even if you're a real gem because you don't know if people will like you for who you are. Let alone I knew I was a fake. I was a failure pretending to be a success.

Nobody knew, but I knew.

I hated myself!

THE UNFOLDING OF MY DESTINY
As the years went by, I decided to go into Finance and Accounting instead of the healthcare industry. It was not by choice. It was because my mark was not high enough. Medicine and Dentistry were beyond my reach. I didn't have the marks. I was not smart enough. I was not good enough.

Accounting was a breeze though. Numbers were always my strong suit. I was back at my old habits, cramming for exams a few days before. And

The Game Changer

deep down, I knew I was not challenged.

I didn't want a job. I didn't want to work for someone else.

I almost walked out on my internship at an accounting firm because I felt I was treated "unfairly." It was an 8-month internship, and I was in my 6th month. I was supposed to do book-keeping/accounting work, but instead, I was reorganizing and cleaning up their archives in a dark storage room in the basement of a building.

I still remember the stench smell of that old storage room. The room was tiny and had only shelves of filing cabinets. It was dim even with the lights on. I hated working down there. I felt scared being there all by myself and I hated how I felt doing that work.

It took me two days working down there to make up my mind. I'm going to talk to my boss, and if he doesn't let me do other work, I'll quit, and the worst-case scenario is I'll just have to redo the eight months internship somewhere else.

I stopped filing, turned off the light and went looking for him.

I don't remember what I said exactly, but I remember quitting and crying at the same time. He must have felt sorry for me, or I might have been too good to let go, but he apologized, and never sent me to the storage room again.

I didn't get it at the time, but my boss didn't do anything wrong. I had finished the "brain" work upstairs, and there was nothing else to do (that I was capable of doing), and I was still on the payroll clock, so he had every right to ask me to go work on the filing cabinets in the basement.

I just couldn't stand it. I couldn't stand doing something I didn't love.

I saw the "catch 22" of working for someone else. You can work hard all you want, but you're still paid by the hour. And when they don't need you anymore, no matter how good you are, they'll still let you go.

I didn't like that environment at all. I wanted more control. I knew I had to be my own boss.

I did, by the way, stay another two months to finish my internship. :)

When I graduated, I continued working at my brother's dental clinic which I started as part-time while taking Accounting school full time for four years.

I had the best and the easiest job anyone could ask for. I was like my own boss. I did the office work, and he did the dental work. I had a six-figure income, but I wasn't happy.

I had a first taste of what it would be like, day in and day out, working at a job that didn't challenge me.

It was too easy, it was too mundane, it was too boring.

I felt dead inside.

It was painful. Not the kind of sharp pain that can help you get out quicker, but it was a dull ache that just kept churning inside, and you just put up with it, you just tolerate.

Until one day, I don't remember how I got this book, but I couldn't put it down. I read it from beginning to end in one night. I didn't even sleep.

The book was "Rich Dad Poor Dad," by Robert Kiyosaki.

It was like I had died that night and was born again. I had a new goal in life.

The Game Changer

"I don't want a career. I don't want a job. I want FREEDOM!"

And the first step to achieving freedom is never to have to worry about money again.

MY JOURNEY TO FREEDOM

To my parents and millions of other Vietnamese who fled Vietnam by boat, that was their journey to freedom. It was a life and death journey, but it was a journey they had to take to survive.

I, too, was on that boat, but that wasn't my fight. I was a child that was well protected, and I felt safe the entire trip. But now as I hear my dad talk about that journey, through his eyes, I realized how hard it really was. We had only three options: prison, death or freedom. We had a "1 out of 3" chance to succeed. Not a very good bet. But it was a bet that we had to take because staying in Vietnam was not an option.

As our boat got out of the Vietnam border and into the international water, we passed the first challenge; we'd escaped Vietnam. Prison was not a worry anymore. But the next hurdle remained until we either reached freedom or we died at sea. Death was always close by but luckily, we made it to freedom.

But that's not the kind of freedom that I dreamed about. That was my parent's journey, not mine.

And now I'm on my own journey to freedom. It's not a matter of life and death literally. But it's a matter of life and death for me. I don't want to die wondering if I had ever lived.

I've targeted a destination called "financial freedom," and I went all in. It was 2003, I was 27, and I wanted to be there in 2010.

I worked hard on it. I attended seminars. I read books. I travelled and learned from many other successful people who had it figured out. I found my path. It was real estate. I believed in it. I believed in myself.

THE RISE TO SUCCESS
I made it!

In just 5 years investing in real estate, I now had over 20 rental properties. I was on top of the world. The market kept shooting up. House prices almost doubled in 3 years. On paper, I was worth at least a few million if I liquidated and sold them all. I was set for life.

I thought I was good. I thought I was smart. This was too easy.

Why should I just stick with buy and hold? Why wouldn't I venture into being a builder? There's so much more money there. I had connections. I had investors. I had guts.

What I really had was GREED.

What I really had was EGO.

I wanted to prove myself to the world. I wanted to show that I'm a badass. Because underneath, I knew I was still a fake. I had a secret. And I was still ashamed of my past.

THE CRASH AND BURN
Greed blinded me. I was opportunistic. I was optimistic. And I paid a hefty price for it.

2008 was the crash of real estate (and everything else for that matter), and I was stuck with 20 rental properties and three newly built infills that alone were worth over 3 million. My total mortgage payments were almost 30k per month. And filling executive suite rentals at that time was extremely challenging.

Talk about regrets and worries! There were nights I wish I could go to sleep and not wake up the next day. I wished I could just vanish from the earth. That was the second time I wish I were dead. Except for this time, it was not about my mom; it was about me. At that time, I already had two sons, a newborn and an 18 months old baby.

In those darkest moments, I thought of killing myself. I was in way over my head. I couldn't handle it. I was trapped. And I have a life insurance policy of 3 million on my head. So if I die, my family would be taken care of. I was worth more to them dead than alive. And I wouldn't have to worry about all the mortgages anymore. The plan was forming in my head.

But my babies were so innocent. They loved me no matter what. They didn't care about my failures. They didn't care about my past.

Somehow they gave me strength. Somehow they gave me courage. I needed them, just as much as they needed me. They gave me a reason to live.

Little by little, one by one, I started to sell off my properties - some were at a big loss. I thought I would make 300k with that one house, but I ended up losing 300k instead.

Somehow I managed, somehow I survived.

But I was lost again.

Not only did I lose all my money, I also lost my identity, again!

I lost my dream.

I lost hope.

THE RECOVERY
Real estate, or the stock market or any types of investments for that matter have their own cycle. Tell me about someone who lost money, and I can

tell you about someone else who made money in that exact market, at that exact time frame. It has little to do with the market but everything to do with the investor. That was my lesson. I had a lot to learn, and I had to do it fast.

My cash flow was so bad that I had to literally strategize which mortgages I had to bounce so that I could get caught up by the next month. It was like I was the hunted, and I had to dodge all these bullets coming at me. And I did, I survived.

I had a bittersweet victory and defeat at the same time. I had it all, and I lost it all. I had gained so much experience, humility, and most of all, humanity.

Have you ever had something really horrible happen to you? And you wish you didn't have to go through all that pain? But a few years later, you realized that was the best thing that ever happened?

I thought I could never recover from my crash and burn but it was the best thing that ever happened to me. It was not easy, but it was necessary. It made me so much stronger. It made me so much wiser. And now I know why I had to go through all that pain. I had to experience this humongous loss so that I can truly appreciate what freedom is all about.

I became more compassionate. I became more forgiving. I became more authentic. I was able to accept me for all my good and bad. I was able to take off my mask. I was able just to be me.
I became "free."

THE REVELATION
Freedom was never about how much money I had in the bank account, or how good I looked. I worked so hard to achieve a certain status that I expected of myself, but I never felt "good enough."

I was never able to accept me for who I really am. I was always trying to be somebody I thought the world wanted me to be.

I was never going to be "good enough" because I didn't like who I was. And I tried to cover it up with what people define "success" to be: fame and fortune.

It was not until I lost it all that I realized my true freedom is the freedom to be ME. And of course, I still have the skills and experiences to pursue my financial freedom again, but this time, I get to do it for me, instead of trying to prove it to the world, or to my mom.

I will never be good enough. And that's ok.

And you will never be good enough. And that's ok.

We have to start somewhere before we can arrive at our destination. We can't be good at anything unless we're willing to suck at it first. Every master was once a disaster.

And you know what the secret is to happiness? Enjoy the journey, honor the struggle and celebrate all along the way.

Don't wait until you're ready. Don't wait until you feel good enough, because it's never good enough!

MY DESTINY

Have you ever heard a story about someone who fought so hard for their dream that they got you so inspired to fight for yours? Have you ever had someone believe in you more than you believed in yourself? Have you ever had someone see the greatness in you when you just couldn't see?

That's what I had when I was going through my toughest time. I had people who I looked up to. I had coaches who believed in me when I didn't. I had coaches who saw the greatness in me when I simply couldn't see.

I had to borrow their lenses for a while until I could see it for myself, until I could truly love myself for who I really am.

And that's what I'm devoting the rest of my life to do. This is my destiny.

I exist so that you feel loved, worthy and good enough. I exist so that people can break free from their mediocre life to create their extraordinary life.

I exist so that anyone can have the true freedom to create anything they want for themselves. I exist so that you can be free from money worries, free from fear of failure and free from feeling inadequate.

So what's your story? What's your dream? What's your destiny? Tell me! I'd love to hear from you.

Shoot me an email at **dreamscometrue@quynhvo.com**, and I'll have a surprise gift waiting for you. :)

To your freedom!

ABOUT THE AUTHOR

What she does in one word is to help you "elevate." No matter where you are, no matter where you've been, and no matter what you do, as long as you "elevate," the universe will conspire to lift you up and take you to places you can only dream of. Places you once thought were impossible and out of reach now become attainable and inevitable.

QUYNH VO is a Freedom Evangelist. She empowers women to step into their greatness and be free from money worries, dead-end jobs, feeling inadequate, a mediocre life.

Most importantly, free to be themselves and be proud of who they are no matter what their background, job, business, appearance, weight, or bank account looks like. You are bound to be successful, bound to be happy and bound to be a free…no matter where you are right now. The only question is: Are you willing to seek support and fight for your dream?

www.quynhvo.com
www.viptaxcare.com

SUSAN BINNIE
You Say You Can't... Think Again! Repeat After Me... Yes, I Can!

There are moments in our lives when we think everything is going to go exactly the way we planned; then we get unexpected news. News that will change everything that we planned for our future. News that is so devastating that you can't be sure if you are more devastated from getting the news or more devastated by how it's going to change the lives around you.

I was pregnant, with my first child, expecting to give birth in early September 1995. Planning the perfect pregnancy, working up to the week before birth. Planning on painting the babies room in August, giving time for everything to be exactly how I pictured it!

Then in mid-July the moment that no one had planned, the moment when my doctor told me that I was going to go to the hospital for observation as my blood pressure was very high. Little did I know that within a week I would give birth to a 4lb 7oz baby girl. My little Angel who would choose me as her mother, would be brought into the world. There wouldn't be time to get her room perfect. No time to have all the things in place that I had planned. I left work early and things changed so rapidly, there was barely time to breathe.

The Game Changer

After you become a mother, typically you bring your baby home from the hospital within a few days. This was not the plan for my little girl and me. She would end up staying in the hospital for the next five weeks. Living between home and the hospital became a way of life for me. Going to the hospital every day, six times a day, to feed her. It was also the time I got to bath her, hold her amd love her. It was a difficult time! Why did she have to be born so early? Why did this have to happen to me? Was there a bigger plan in store?

None of this was planned, life was not supposed to be this way. I had no time to think, sleep or breathe. I was upset every moment and just wanted to curl up into a ball and cry. Finally, after five very long and emotional weeks, she was strong enough to come home, strong enough to be the normal little girl that would have a perfect life. The life I had planned for her.

She had to pass a car seat study to prove that she could make the ride home. The nurses pushed her through the test, knowing that she would be loved and cared for. Test after test, after retest, they finally told me it was time to take her home. I arrived the next morning to take my precious baby home, to hear the unthinkable news...news that I can still hear so clearly, just like it was yesterday. "Your daughter's head grew a centimeter overnight. We believe she has hydrocephalus, water on the brain. The neurosurgeon has been consulted and will be here shortly to speak to you about your daughters' condition."

"My daughter what???" "Her head what???" "She has what???" Then in a blink of an eye, it happened, that moment, that devastating moment that would change our lives forever. I was full of tears, and more emotional stress than I ever thought possible. The doctor said she could come home. I just had to measure her head four times a day to make sure it was not getting any bigger.

I will never forget those moments of measuring her head looking at the measuring tape through tears and hoping that it would get smaller instead of larger. I don't remember sleeping; I was so scared she was going to die. I slept with one eye opened and one eye closed for the next few days. Her head was not getting any smaller, and the neurosurgeon decided to do surgery within the week. She received a VP shunt, a valve put in her brain that would drain fluid from her ventricles in her brain down into her tummy cavity...getting absorbed within her system.

I was told she could still have a completely normal life. The doctors did not know exactly how things would be for her, but she would survive and grow and get stronger just like any child of her size. She may need numerous surgeries throughout life to revise the valve and the tubing, but all things considered, she was doing well. I finally could take her home and live life as normally as humanly possible. I was not sure what normal meant and how I would deal with all the emotions I had. I remember many tears and so many moments that I blamed myself as somehow this must be my fault. How do I take care of her I thought? How do I...I can't, I just can't!

Having a child changes a life, there is no doubt about it. Anyone who has ever had a child can tell you that. A little human that completely comes to rely on you to be there every moment in life! Life for us was going to be a little more chaotic than that of someone with a child that does not have a shunt. It may get blocked, may stop working, may need to be replaced. The doctor told us that common cold symptom, could be that of the shunt not working. There were many questions in my mind; How would I know when there was a problem for sure? Would it be an emergency? Could this kill her?

Over the months that followed everything seemed reasonably normal. A little baby, doing all of the things babies do, and a mother taking care of things a typical mother would do. Doctor's appointments became part of the normal routine, weekly at first, then monthly. When she was six months old, I noticed that her left side was not the same as her right. What now? I thought. Her left side seemed weaker; it did not move as quickly, perhaps it was just because she was right-handed.

The Game Changer

At her six months checkup, I asked the doctor about her motor skills, her weakness on her left side, the noticeable difference…it did not take him long to confirm what I had suspected. The devastating news no mother ever wants to hear, and I was about to hear it for the second time. "Your child has a disability."

At first, my brain immediately thought, yes she has Hydrocephalus. But, I already knew that. Then I heard it, "Your daughter has Cerebral Palsy!" Her left side was affected, and they did not know exactly how severe it would be until she started to grow. Cerebral Palsy affects everyone differently. The brain does not tell the muscles to grow at the same rate as everything else. The higher up her limbs the disease was, the more disabled she would be.

What did life have in store now? The sleepless nights of worry, the special adaptations, physical therapy, special schooling, and all the other things we didn't even know to ask. I lost track of how many times we went to the emergency department believing her shunt was causing a problem. The times she was sick, pale as a ghost and did not do anything but cry. It was very difficult seeing the doctors and nurses trying to take blood making her pain worse. Seeing her have all the x-rays and CT scans that would not show any results to warrant that she was severe enough for them to do anything for her.

Over the years things became very difficult for her, for us and all of those who would help her. The word can't have become one of the most defining words in Angela's life, but I had no idea how prominent it would be in mine. As she started to grow and do things differently than normal children of her age, the whole world of cant's started to happen. The therapists and doctors told us many things that she could not do. She can't crawl. She can't use her left hand for fine motor skills. She can't use her left arm properly; her gross motor skills will be affected. She can't walk without a brace. She can't dress herself like other children. She can't eat by herself; she can't go to normal school like other children. The list went on and on. Bottom line, she can't do things like other kids. She is different; she has special needs!

Susan Binnie: You Say You Can't...Think Again!...Repeat After Me...

When Angela was very young, I knew there was only one option. The word "can't" must be removed from her life. I was tired of hearing all the things she would never do. As a mother, it was very hard to continue hearing all the things wrong with my child. It reminded me of when I was told all the things I can't or shouldn't do. I was 18 and was told I needed back surgery due to a protruding disc. Surgery was the only option.

During recovery, the back specialist told me all the things I would never be able to do, or shouldn't including sports, lifting heavy objects, "oh, and you should never have children, your body will not be able to handle it." Looking back, I am very glad I did not listen to the doctor. I was very stubborn; I played baseball and soccer, I installed carpet and went on to have two children. The doctor had no idea what my life would be for sure and what I could or could not do.

I have come to realize that anything you want bad enough in this world, you just find a way. It might be a different way than anyone else, you just figure out how, and do it.

For Angela, this would be no different. Sure, the things she did would look very different than how typically they are done, but she would always be taught that she can do anything she wants to do in life. The harder you work for things, the more they will mean. "Can't" will not be part of her life.

As the years went on, she learned that things were different for her and they always would be. She wore a specially molded brace on her hand and her foot, she spent countless hours learning to hold cutlery to feed herself & she walked before she crawled. Angela wore Velcro shoes for many years of her life and when she was finally ready to learn how to tie her shoes the one-handed way, she refused to learn. She wanted to learn with both hands.

It was not easy, but she fought and fought and finally found a way that worked for her. She went through life beating all the odds. Doing things, she wanted, when she wanted. She rode a bike with special adaptations and training wheels until the bike was too big for training wheels. Then she just decided she did not want to ride anymore.

Angela was in some form of school from the time she was 3. She would need to learn things in a special way. We enrolled her into a special school and this was the time I decided it was time for me to find a job that could accommodate me starting later than everyone else, to allow me time to take her to school. Flexible enough for me to be able to take 1.5-hour lunch breaks, with time to pick her up, get her to her daycare, and time to eat lunch. Then the ability to work a little later, so I would still put in the same 8-hour day as everyone else. I started a job at a not-for-profit health organization. They soon came to realize that I was a very valuable employee and would go above and beyond to prove how dedicated I was to the organization. Unconsciously I feel I did this to pay back for the flexibility they gave me.

Days turned into weeks and weeks turned into years. After seven years I decided that this job had become my second home. It provided the flexibility I needed to be there for Angela through every stage of her life. She had been going to school in a normal setting and taking the bus to and from school from my sisters. I decided it was time to take on more responsibility within the foundation. Sure, it would mean some late nights and some weekends, but it was totally worth it.

My role had changed several times. I was helping with special events and had taken on the task of speaking and educating groups. Before long I realized that I wanted more than what the job had to offer. How could I leave, I felt so stuck...I had more responsibilities at home, and I continued to need the flexibility for doctor's appointments, surgeries and caregiver duties.

2010 would prove to be one of the most difficult years for Angela and me. Her shunt was blocked. She was in awful pain, but unfortunately, all the medical tests did not show there was any medically evidenced proof that there was a problem. When she was upright, the swelling and pain got worse. She spent many hours in bed feeling very sick. After many long appointments crying in doctors' offices trying to figure out how I would help my little girl, the neurosurgeon finally agreed to do surgery. As a mother, there is nothing worse than hearing, "mommy take the pain away."

My answer every time through teary eyes, and a sore, heavy chest was, "I can't sweetheart; I don't know how." Being scared, and remembering how I felt that all of this must be my fault somehow and allowing the fear to take over. Priorities in life changed and I had more responsibilities at home. Time became so precious for all of us. I needed to spend more time focusing on what was most important, and work became less and less of a place I wanted to be.

I had been at the foundation for 12 years and realized I took on many tasks that were never in my job description. I helped my colleagues where ever I was asked. I forgot the word "NO" was even an option. I stayed at first because I wanted to be there, but now I can't go work elsewhere I thought. I have no choice. I was afraid of change. I can't leave, how could I ever replace the income I got, and the benefits, the pension, and the security.

Over the years I worked so hard taking the word can't out of Angela's life. The problem was, I didn't take the word can't out of my life. Work had become just a job, and the passion I had for what I was doing was no longer in me.

I thought, how could this have happened?

Easy. The same way things happen when you don't have a plan, you don't set goals, you don't have a vision or passion for what your future will look like!

Every day I helped my daughter overcome many obstacles in her life. At the same time, I was allowing myself to be beaten down mentally, and emotionally. After a few years, I believed it when anyone said, "you can't write a decent letter," "you can't run an event your way," "you must do it our way," "you can't speak about what you want from your heart," and, "you must do it our way, with stats, risk factors, and figures." Over time I lost my self-worth, my confidence and my sense of being. I heard and felt can't and believed in my head and my heart, I could not!

I was feeling very stuck at work at the same time Angela was making her way through school. Schooling was adapted for her through the years as her cognitive ability was affected. In grade 12 it took her a little more time to complete the final exams, but she graduated from high school at the same age as all her friends. I felt so proud of her when she graduated! She had a disability, or two, and had since been diagnosed with an autoimmune disease. How did I manage to do such a great job with her and keep the word can't out of her life while I had it in mine and felt so stuck?

I am one of the women in the world who was under the misbelief that if I did not have the job I was destined to have by the time I was 50, then life was over. Once my children move out my purpose is done at home, and all that is left is my career. In August 2015, months before my 49th birthday, I was downsized after 17 years of employment. Now, what do I have, 50 is around the corner; my youngest will soon be old enough she will want to leave. Life as I know it is over! I truly believed my purpose was over. There are so many things I can't do.

Then I remembered what I always told my daughter!

You can do whatever you want in life if you want it bad enough. Figure out a way; there is a way for you, you just must find it, or be patient enough for it to find you.

I am a wife, a mother and a grandmother. Not just a person, an employee, a number. I am a human being, and I have family that needs me. But is that enough? How will I to survive? What will I do to get paid?

Fortunately, I had almost two years to figure it out. During this time, I

Susan Binnie: You Say You Can't?...Think Again! Repeat After Me...

was called by God to fulfill a higher calling. Called to empower women to take the word can't out of their life so they can have the life they want, the life they are destined to have and feel great about what they choose to do in the process!

Life teaches us many things! Some things we remember better than others. Some things we need to learn over and over before we can make any sense of them and some things just happen without any reason that we can figure out.

One thing I know for sure is that I was lost for many years not realizing that I had choices. Choices that could have made things easier for me, choices that could have stopped the fear and stopped the worry. What I have come to appreciate is that everything happens for a reason and it does not have to take a lifetime of being lost to figure it out, sometimes you just need to let go of the fear and ask for help!

If I asked for help sooner, and looked harder for a way to take the word can't out of my life, things would have turned out much differently. I was down-sized for a reason. I consistently figure out how to take the word can't out of my life and empower women to take the word can't out of their lives so they can have the life they want. Life is too short to be spinning your wheels doing what you don't want or what you think you can't. Everyone should live their dream and not get stuck in the middle of someone else's vision for the future.

I feel so blessed to live my passion and feel empowered myself when I empower other women to create a path they will be proud to travel on through their journey of LIFE! Tell yourself every day...YES, I CAN!

Yes U Can...
Yes U Will...
Cause Yes You Are...
Cause Yes You Can!
Susan
What everyone say you are!

ABOUT THE AUTHOR

SUSAN BINNIE started her professional career when she was 18. Starting in the administrative world, she soon became part of the sales team, then the management team. A natural born leader for over 30 years. Throughout corporate downsizing in Alberta Canada, Susan decided to make a difference in the health industry for a not for profit organization. Through her fundraising efforts, she supported many lives affected by heart disease and stroke.

Susan learned to speak from her heart five years ago as it related to her work with the research efforts she helped fund which also benefited her family directly, and realized along the way that she has a bigger purpose on earth! Susan is an entrepreneur, motivational speaker and most importantly the mother of 4 amazing children.

Against all the odds, she started her business as a motivational speaker just a year ago and today speaks on several stages every month. She also runs workshops for women who want to achieve massive success by believing in their power without getting overwhelmed. Susan is also the founder of the International Women's Empowerment Network.

Stay Connected.
Thanks for being a part of my journey!

First book
in
The Game Changer Series

Get Your Copy Today!
http://amzn.to/2Gh3M2V

Made in the USA
Columbia, SC
30 April 2018